FOUR WEEKS IN MAY

FOUR WEEKS IN MAY

The Loss of HMS Coventry
A Captain's Story

DAVID HART DYKE

Atlantic Books
London

First published in Great Britain in 2007 by Atlantic Books,
an imprint of Grove Atlantic Ltd

3 5 7 9 8 6 4 2

A CIP catalogue record for this book is available from the British Library.

ISBN 978 1 84354 590 3

Maps and graphics © Mark Rolfe Technical Art

Images of Firth of Forth and Turning South for the Falklands © Crown Copyright/MOD.
Reproduced with the permission of the Controller of Her Majesty's Stationery Office.

Extract from *One Hundred Days* by Alexander Woodward reprinted by permission
of HarperCollins Publishers Ltd © Alexander Woodward with Patrick Robinson 1992

Extract from *Memories of the Falklands* by Iain Dale (ed)
reproduced by permission of the author © Margaret Thatcher 2002

Printed in Great Britain by MPG Books Ltd, Bodmin, Cornwall

Atlantic Books
An imprint of Grove Atlantic Ltd.
Ormond House
26–27 Boswell Street
London WC1N 3JZ

For the Ship's Company of HMS *Coventry* 1982
and, of course, D

CONTENTS

ILLUSTRATIONS

MAPS AND DIAGRAMS

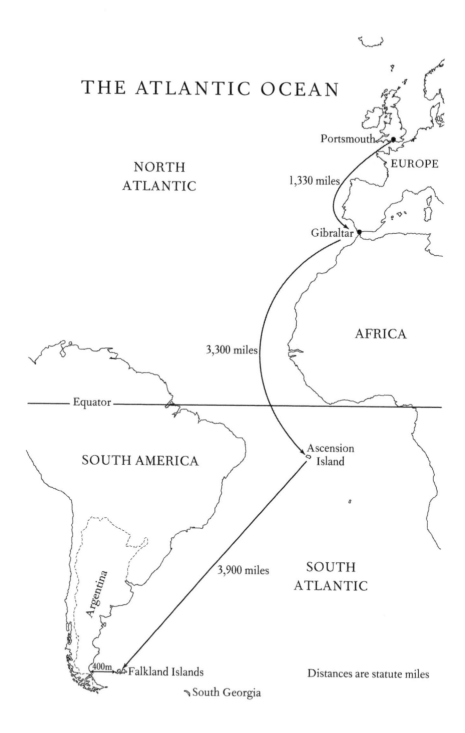

THE ATLANTIC OCEAN

NORTH
ATLANTIC

Portsmouth

EUROPE

1,330 miles

Gibraltar

AFRICA

3,300 miles

Equator

SOUTH AMERICA

Ascension
Island

Argentina

3,900 miles

SOUTH
ATLANTIC

400m Falkland Islands

South Georgia

Distances are statute miles

ARGENTINIAN AIR
AND NAVAL BASES

ARGENTINA

CHILE

Buenos Aires

Espora
Puerto Belgrano

Coronel

Trelew

0   200

Statute Miles

N

Comodoro Rivadavia

Puerto Deseado
San Julian
Santa Cruz

Mirage

Skyhawk

Super Etendard

Rio Gallegos

Port Stanley

Punta
Arenas

Rio Grande

Total Exclusion
Zone

Ushuaia

450m   575m 625m
Unrefuelled maximum
radii of action

DISPOSITION OF FORCES BEFORE
EXOCET ATTACK, 4 MAY

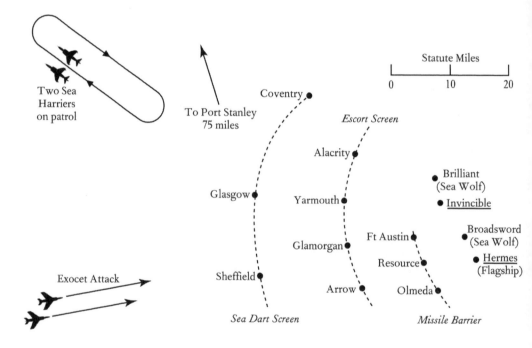

Two Sea
Harriers
on patrol

To Port Stanley
75 miles

Statute Miles

0   10   20

Coventry

Escort Screen

Alacrity

Brilliant
(Sea Wolf)

Glasgow

Yarmouth

● Invincible

Broadsword
(Sea Wolf)

Ft Austin

Glamorgan

● Hermes
(Flagship)

Resource

Exocet Attack

Sheffield

Arrow

Olmeda

Sea Dart Screen

Missile Barrier

SHIP LOSSES, MAY 1982

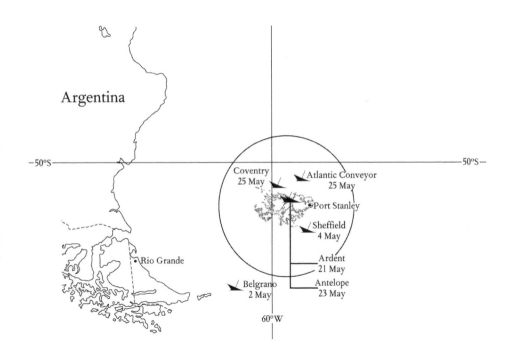

Argentina

−50°S

Coventry
25 May

Atlantic Conveyor
25 May

Port Stanley

Sheffield
4 May

Ardent
21 May

Antelope
23 May

Belgrano
2 May

Rio Grande

50°S

60°W

THE FALKLAND ISLANDS

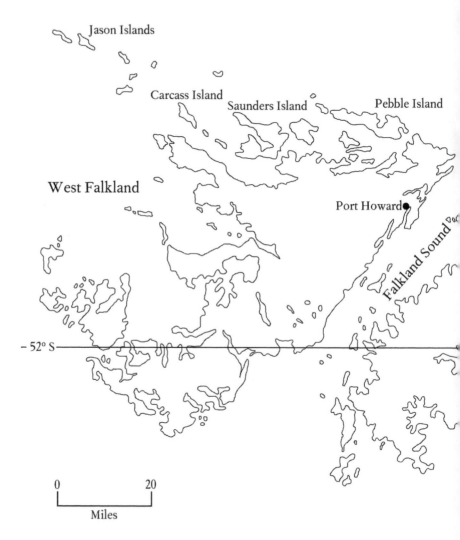

Jason Islands

Carcass Island

Saunders Island

Pebble Island

West Falkland

Port Howard

Falkland Sound

– 52° S

0   20

Miles

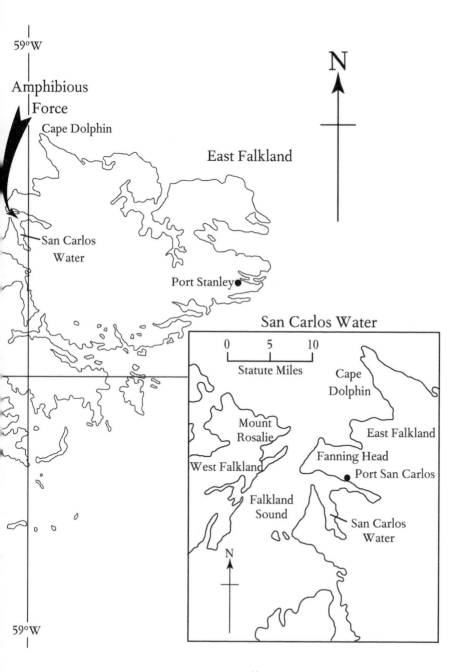

59°W

Amphibious
Force

Cape Dolphin

East Falkland

N

San Carlos
Water

Port Stanley●

San Carlos Water

0   5   10

Statute Miles

Cape
Dolphin

Mount
Rosalie

East Falkland

Fanning Head

West Falkland

● Port San Carlos

Falkland
Sound

San Carlos
Water

N

59°W

TASK FORCE COMMAND AND CONTROL

LONDON

The Prime Minister
Rt Hon Margaret Thatcher MP

The Secretary of State for Defence
Rt Hon John Nott MP

Chief of the Defence Staff
Admiral of the Fleet Sir Terence Lewin

Chief of Naval Staff and First Sea Lord
Admiral Sir Henry Leach

Chief of the General Staff
General Sir Edwin Bramall

Chief of the Air Staff
Air Chief Marshal Sir Michael Beetham

NORTHWOOD

Task Force Commander
Admiral Sir John Fieldhouse

Flag Officer Submarines	Land Deputy	Chief of Staff	Air Force Commander
Vice Admiral	*Major General*	*Vice Admiral*	*Air Marshal*
P. G. M. Herbert	*J. J. Moore*	*D. J. Hallifax*	*Sir John Curtiss*
	(Later Commander		
	Land Forces, Falkland Islands)		

FALKLANDS

Carrier Battle Group	Amphibious Task Group	Landing Force Group
Rear Admiral	*Commodore*	*Brigadier*
J. F. Woodward	*M. C. Clapp*	*J. H. A. Thompson*
(Embarked in	(Embarked in	(Commanding 3
HMS *Hermes*)	HMS *Fearless*)	Commando Brigade)

ACKNOWLEDGEMENTS

This book became a serious project after author Patrick Robinson and Dr Campbell McMurray, the Director of the Royal Naval Museum, Portsmouth, had seen an early draft and considered it worthy of publication. I am grateful to them for their encouragement, since, without it, these pages would have just gathered dust at home.

I wish to thank my daughter Miranda for providing the necessary spur to start me writing by making a transcript of the tapes I made on which the book is based. Thanks are also due to my younger daughter Alice, Sir Michael Jenkins, Vice-Admiral Sir John Webster, Captain Michael Barrow, Major-General Julian Thompson and Admiral Sir Sandy Woodward for their advice and comment.

I am indebted to Toby Mundy, Angus MacKinnon and Emma Grove of Atlantic Books for their unfailing support and enthusiasm; Angus deserves particular thanks for his meticulous and skilful editing.

Finally, I thank my agent, James Gill, who guided me so

professionally all the way to publication. Nothing would have happened without him.

My wife D deserves special praise for both her important contribution to the book and for living through the dramatic events of 1982 with remarkable calm and strength.

PREFACE

In March 1982, a group of Argentinians raised their flag in South Georgia and started a dramatic chain of events. On 2 April, Argentinian troops invaded the Falkland Islands and later South Georgia. The small British garrison of Royal Marines was overwhelmed by the vastly superior number of invaders.

By 5 April, the main components of a British Carrier Battle Group had set sail for the South Atlantic. A few days earlier, a flotilla of ships exercising off Gibraltar under the command of Rear Admiral Sandy Woodward had been ordered to sail south in advance of the main force. HMS *Coventry* was part of this advance group. Diplomatic efforts, supported by a United Nations resolution, failed to persuade Argentina to remove its occupying troops.

South Georgia was reoccupied after a brief encounter with the Argentinian garrison on 25 April. A number of fierce engagements followed in the war zone surrounding the Falkland Islands. On 21 May, some 5,000 British troops stormed ashore at San Carlos Bay and established a bridgehead, from where they advanced to Darwin and Goose Green. A further thrust took place at Bluff Cove and the advance towards Port Stanley, the capital, began in earnest.

Almost all the high ground around Stanley was in British hands by 12 June and the routed Argentinians fell back into Stanley. On 14 June, their commander surrendered his forces and the commander of the British land forces reported: 'The Falkland Islands are once more under the Government desired by their inhabitants. God Save the Queen.'

Four Weeks in May is the story of the guided-missile destroyer *Coventry*, which made a significant contribution to this remarkable victory, achieved against very considerable odds 8,000 miles from home, and which in the end went down fighting against bomber aircraft. It is also the story of the ship's company, who fought a dangerous, arduous and intense battle in one of the most inhospitable regions of the world with great courage and endurance. And lastly, it is my own story as *Coventry's* captain. It was my privilege to lead such brave men in battle and they are, quite simply, my heroes.

Many people who have suffered in war do not care to talk about their experiences because, when they do, they relive them intensely – as if these events had happened only yesterday, not years or decades earlier. Some go to their graves without ever feeling able to describe or discuss what they went through, even with close friends or family. I was lucky: over time, I learnt to shut out the more painful memories and to live more easily with them. And I wanted to tell *Coventry's* story before I got too old, even if my descendants would only read it after stumbling across these pages in the attic.

My account is largely based on tapes which I made soon after

I returned from the South Atlantic. Even now, I can hear myself speaking into the microphone in a distinctly flat voice as I began to recover at home from the traumas of the war: I simply wanted to set down a record of events and my impressions of them while both remained fresh in my memory. I have never wished to listen to those tapes since, but I have had them transcribed. I have also made use of the letters my wife and I exchanged during the conflict. In addition, I have drawn on articles I wrote in the autumn of 1982 for various naval publications recounting my experiences, contemporary newspaper accounts of the conflict that I kept, and the reminiscences of some of my former crew members. These reminiscences, which come from diaries kept at the time or accounts written later, were offered to me when I made it known that I was writing this book and seeking contributions.

I hardly comment on the broader strategy of the campaign and the tactics employed: where I do, it is only as they affected me as one of the commanding officers of the ships operating in the front line. I do not wish otherwise to pronounce on the conduct of the war. This is not a history book: it is the story of the war at sea as I saw it in *Coventry* and as I recorded it back in 1982.

I write about one warship and its men, but there were over forty others in the campaign whose daring exploits would make compelling reading. I have an undying admiration for those ships and their crews, especially the ones *Coventry* was fortunate to work with closely, and I hope that *Four Weeks in May* goes some way towards showing how magnificently they performed in this most testing of wars. Their hardships and their fears were at least as great as mine, and they faced them with the utmost resolve.

I have mentioned some of my former crew members by name but there are many others whom I remember well and would have included had space allowed. I only hope that this book pays sufficient tribute to everyone on board, for I do not know of a single person in the ship who did not excel in his duties and live up to the fighting tradition of the Royal Navy. It is, after all, not ships, aircraft and weapons that win wars, but people. And this story is all about people.

Hambledon, 2006

HMS *COVENTRY*
BATTLE HONOURS

Quiberon 1759	Greece 1941
Trincomalee 1782	Crete 1941
Spartivento 1940	Libya 1941
Atlantic 1940	Mediterranean 1941
Norway 1940	Falkland Islands 1982

The name of *Coventry* is an illustrious one in Royal Navy history going back to the seventeenth century. The battle honours show HMS *Coventry*'s long and active history, and in more recent times there has been a proud association between the city and the ship.

The fourth HMS *Coventry* was completed in 1918 and later converted into an anti-aircraft cruiser with high-angle 4-inch guns. In 1941 she joined the desperate fighting in the Mediterranean and shot down more enemy aircraft than most other ships. In September 1942 she was bombed and sunk off Tobruk.

The fifth HMS *Coventry*, an anti-aircraft destroyer, entered service in 1979 and, much like her predecessor, distinguished herself by destroying more aircraft than others, either with her own missiles or by radar control, during the Falklands War. On 25 May she came under heavy attack and was struck by three bombs. In seconds she was on fire, flooding and listing rapidly. She was abandoned with the loss of nineteen men – but not before several of her crew had crawled in darkness and toxic fumes to check for anyone alive. They brought many to safety.

FOUR WEEKS IN MAY

APOCALYPSE

During the last few hectic days of the conflict, we all realized that the odds of emerging unscathed were stacked against us. We always knew that we might be hit from the air – it was just a question of where and of how many casualties we would sustain. After all, three warships had already been sunk and others damaged. I frequently thought along these lines and I am sure most of my sailors did, but we never admitted it openly. That would have been demoralizing. Conversations were brave and cheerful, full of confidence that we would all get home safely. We were all strengthened by such talk and by the bold banter and good humour among colleagues, however much we inwardly believed that some of us might never get back.

I was shocked when, a day or two before the end, the first lieu-tenant, the second-in-command, came into my cabin and with noticeable hesitation said, 'You know, sir, some of us are not going to get back to Portsmouth.' Although it disturbed me to hear him say this, I thought it was very brave of him to admit to his captain what he really felt, and at least we no longer had to pretend to each other about the risks we were running. He included himself among those who would not return and in his last letter home he told his wife as much. She was to receive the letter just after she heard the news that he had been killed.

Towards the end of our time, the strains were definitely beginning to tell. Although most people remained outwardly strong and in control of themselves, feelings clearly ran high. Once, quite unprompted, a young sailor on the bridge showed me photographs of his girlfriend and talked freely about her. He was in need of reassurance and this was his way of showing it. There had already been air raids that day, and we knew the enemy would be among us again very soon. On a similar occasion, a petty officer produced a prayer, given to him by his mother when he first joined the Navy, which he kept with him all the time and which clearly meant a great deal to him, especially now. He asked me to read it in our church service on Sunday and then moved quickly out on to the wings of the bridge for fear of showing the tears in his eyes. War can be an emotional business.

I found it depressing to wake each morning to beautiful, clear and sunny weather which favoured the enemy air force and illuminated us sharply against the blue sea. I would wait on the bridge, heavily clothed for protection against fire, lifejacket and survival suit around my waist, ready for the next air raid warning. When it came, I would go down to the operations room to prepare to counter the threat. These moments invariably demanded a certain amount of nerve: you had to put on a confident face as men watched you go below and wondered whether we would win the next round and survive unharmed.

Tuesday, 25 May 1982, was another of those days. We had

survived two air raids and shot down three aircraft with missiles. Inevitably, there was another warning and I went below feeling more fearful than before. I paused for a moment at the top of the hatch and talked briefly to Lieutenant Rod Heath, the officer responsible for the missile system. I never saw him again. At 6 p.m. precisely, I pressed the action-station alarm from the command position in the operations room and within four minutes the ship was closed down, ready and braced for action.

As we listened to the air battle raging, we tried desperately to avoid losing radar contact with the fast and low-flying enemy aircraft and to predict where they were going next. Once again, it was a question of split-second timing, and I had to decide whether to guide our Sea Harrier fighter aircraft to intercept or to bring the ship's missile system to bear. There was the familiar air of quiet professionalism, the sound of keyboards as operators tracked targets and of soft but urgent voices exchanging information over the internal lines. It was like some frantic computer game, and we knew we would lose the battle if we could not keep up with its ever-quickening pace. As I glanced around at the warfare team, their pale and anxious faces said everything. I looked at the clock – it was nearly 6.15 p.m. – and prayed that time would somehow accelerate, enabling us to see out what would be the last air raid of the day. Even now, I knew that outside in the South Atlantic the light was already beginning to fade, the prelude to another brilliant sunset.

As it was, we came up against a very brave and determined attack by four Argentinian aircraft. We opened fire with everything we had, from Sea Dart missiles to machine guns and even rifles, but two aircraft got through, hitting us with three 1,000-pound bombs, two of which exploded deep down inside the ship.

The severe damage caused immediate flooding and fire, and all power and communications were lost. Within about twenty minutes, the ship was upside down, her keel horizontal a few feet above the sea. Tragically, nineteen men were killed, most by the blast of the bombs. Yet it still strikes me as remarkable that some 280 of us got out of the ship, whose interior was devastated and filled with thick, suffocating smoke. I can only put that down to good training, discipline and high morale. You need all of these, especially the last, in desperate situations.

My own world simply stopped. I was aware of a flash, of heat and the crackling of the radar set as it literally disintegrated in front of my face. When I came to my senses, I could see nothing through the dense black smoke, only people on fire, but I could sense that the compartment had been totally devastated. Those who were able to take charge did so calmly and effectively. It seemed like an age, but when you are fighting for your life, the brain speeds up and time slows down: the focus of your thoughts narrows and you concentrate on just one thing – survival. At such times, pain, injury and even freezing seas are not even distractions; they simply do not enter into your calculations.

I was two decks down and had a long way to go to reach fresh air. I could see no way out and was suffocating in the smoke. The ladders were gone and doors were blocked by fire. I was calm and not at all frightened. I was feeling quite rational and was prepared to die. There seemed to be no alternative.

CHAPTER 1

BEFORE
THE STORM

I was fortunate to be married to someone who had a naval background and therefore understood the life of a sea-going naval officer and the necessary separations involved. Although my wife's father was a diplomat, one who had served abroad for most of his life, her great-grandfather, great-uncle, both grandfathers and an uncle were all admirals. One of her grandfathers, John Luce, was the captain of the light cruiser *Glasgow* in the Battle of the Falklands in 1914. A lucky ship, *Glasgow* had survived the earlier defeat of a British squadron by the Germans off the Chilean coast at Coronel.

I first encountered Diana – known by family and friends as just D – while serving in the frigate *Gurkha* in the Persian Gulf in 1966. Her father, Sir William Luce, was the Political Resident in Bahrain with responsibilities for the Gulf, and just before he retired we took him to sea to call on all the region's rulers and sheikhs, beginning with Kuwait and ending in Oman in the port of Muscat. Sir William had been granted permission to take his daughter and his social secretary, Vicky Vigors, on the three-day trip, although he had been advised not to inform the First Sea Lord, who happened to be his brother, Admiral Sir David Luce.

The two girls slept in the first lieutenant's cabin with a Royal Marine on guard outside throughout the night, and they spent a great deal of time during the day sunbathing in bikinis on the teak deck just below and in front of the bridge. There was no shortage of volunteers to keep watch on the bridge and it was noticeable that their binoculars were not exactly fixed on the far horizon looking for ships. My own efforts at pretending not to approve of women at sea did not last long as one day D asked me if I could show her where we were on the chart. I was *Gurkha*'s navigator, but replied that I had absolutely no idea, throwing the rubber on to the chart and adding that we were probably just about where it landed. This rather relaxed and nonchalant approach to navigation clearly did the trick, however, as we were married eighteen months later.

My naval connections could not compare with D's. My father was a naval officer who joined at the age of thirteen in the early 1920s and served throughout the Second World War, mainly in the Atlantic. He retired shortly after the war, went into the Church and became parish priest of the village of Cowden in Kent. He died in 1971 while on a working holiday on the West Indian island of Nevis: he had been running the church there to allow the incumbent to return home to England for a short break.

In 1976, when I was the commander of the destroyer *Hampshire*, we passed Nevis on our way to Trinidad but did not have time to stop. I was none the less able to fly to the island in the ship's helicopter to pay a very brief visit to my father's grave. I descended from the helicopter in my white uniform and began to walk the short distance to the church. As I did so, I quickly found myself being followed by a large number of excited local people. They continued to follow me with great curiosity wherever I went – to the church, the grave and to the rectory where my father stayed. I was puzzled at first, but it transpired that the members of this small, church-going community thought I actually was my father, now resurrected and descending from the heavens to visit them once again. The confusion was perhaps understandable: I resemble my father, and my white uniform could well have been taken for the white cassock that he habitually wore in Nevis. Eventually, I was bid a sad farewell, as if I were him, from hundreds of well-wishers while I waved goodbye from the helicopter before it lifted off and returned to the heavens. It was an emotional visit.

There have been only two other naval Hart Dykes as far as I am aware. Henry was a midshipman who in the 1850s served in *Agamemnon*, the first ship of the line to be powered by both sail and steam, and he retired as a rear admiral, while Wyndham ended his career with the rank of commander after serving in both world wars. My Hart Dyke grandfather served in the Indian Army, winning a DSO in the First World War, and my father's elder brother also had a distinguished career in the Army, winning a DSO in the Second.

Among my mother's family, the Alexanders, were some very good artists, my mother being one and her uncle Herbert another. Two of her other Alexander uncles, Boyd of the Rifle Brigade and Claud of the Scots Guards, became famous explorers and naturalists whose exploits in Africa in the early twentieth century are recorded in the two volumes of *From the Niger to the Nile*, written by Boyd in 1907. Boyd had a twin brother, Robert, my mother's father. In 1910 Herbert was asked by Captain Scott to go on his expedition to the South Pole as the artist but his father would not let him go as he did not want to risk losing another son. In 1904 Claud had succumbed to blackwater fever in Africa and Boyd was killed six years later by tribesmen near Lake Chad in northern Nigeria, an area he largely discovered and mapped. Edward Wilson went with Scott to the Pole instead. The Alexander genes gave me both an interest in painting – in my case watercolours – and also a twin brother, Robert.

As a naval officer's son, during my formative years I thought only of the Navy as a career, though near the end of my schooldays I was diverted towards university. It was not possible at that time to join the Navy as a seaman officer after university; the service wanted to educate its officer recruits straight from school in its own way – broadly, in the ways of the sea and following a more technical curriculum. A degree course in an arts subject was probably considered more of an obstacle than an attribute when it came to moulding people into naval officers at Dartmouth. After missing the chance to join the Navy from school, I then declined to go to university and waited for the call to do national service. I saw an opportunity of gaining a commission in the Navy during my national service and then, or so I hoped, becoming a regular officer. National service itself was almost at an end, and it was a risky plan. But it worked, and I arrived at Dartmouth about two years older than my contemporaries and after I had spent a year at sea as a midshipman.

After Dartmouth, I spent many years at sea, mostly in destroyers and frigates, projecting the United Kingdom's interests around the world and helping to make it a more stable place. I passionately believed in this important role, one in which, after centuries of experience, the Royal Navy was highly effective. I specialized in navigation, an area which embraced warfare in all its forms and the conduct of operations. By the nature of the job, I was always close to the commanding officer: I was responsible for the safe navigation of the ship and also ran the operations room when we were practising for war. I was therefore well trained for command when the time came. In addition, I had held two teaching posts, one at Dartmouth and the other at the Naval Staff College in Greenwich. Following my time at the Staff College, I was fortunate to be appointed the commander of the royal yacht *Britannia* for two years and so witnessed at first hand the impact the vessel made with the Queen embarked as it visited various heads of state abroad, earning much goodwill and valuable trade agreements for the UK.

I was given command of the modern guided-missile destroyer *Coventry* in 1981 after twenty-two years of very enjoyable and rewarding appointments. We were to be busy at sea from the day I joined, and I soon found that I had inherited a well-run and efficient ship – something which had not always been my experience. *Coventry* spent time with the Standing Naval Force Atlantic, a squadron of NATO ships, and took part in a major exercise in the North Sea. Then, in the spring of 1982, she was to depart on what proved to be her final voyage.

We sailed from Portsmouth in the middle of March in company with *Antrim*, flagship of the Flag Officer of the First Flotilla, Rear Admiral J. F. 'Sandy' Woodward, to meet up with other ships departing from Plymouth. We then set course as a group for Gibraltar, which was to be our base as we carried out a number of routine weapons-training exercises, including missile firings. We would take advantage of the various training facilities ashore and the practice targets at sea, provided by both submarines and aircraft, to practise our war-fighting skills. There would also be sporting and social activities for ships' companies – opportunities for all to catch up with friends and to compare notes with other ships. It all seemed perfectly straight-forward: a standard period of springtime exercises for ships based in home waters.

In Gibraltar, *Coventry* was berthed alongside *Glasgow*, our friendly sister ship. Paul Hoddinot, the captain, came on board for a drink and a chat with me, and there were similar comings and goings between friends at other levels in both ships. Paul was a near contemporary of mine but his background was in submarines and so I did not know him all that well. He seemed quietly confident, impressive and very likeable. I thought it would be fun to be working with him and his ship, which was clearly a good one.

I learnt later that some of his sailors had taken the tompion off *Coventry*'s 4.5-inch gun as a prank and had taken it back on board *Glasgow* as a trophy. This stainless steel cylinder carries the ship's crest on one end and slides over the gun to help make everything look smart when entering and leaving harbour; it also prevents rain, sea and spray from getting inside the barrel. No doubt it would have been given back when the ships met up again. As it was, I had no idea the tompion was even missing until after the war, when Paul came to see me at home in Hampshire and presented me with it. Thus it survived and is now a valued memento which acts as a rather original doorstop.

Another of our sister ships, *Sheffield*, with Captain Sam Salt in command, glided gracefully into harbour looking very smart and purposeful. I went on board to see Sam and hear all his news. He was a friend from several years before when our paths had crossed during various training courses in Portsmouth, and he was always good fun and a thorough professional. Everyone loved working for Sam and he ran a very happy and efficient ship.

The three Type 42 destroyers (*Coventry*, *Glasgow* and *Sheffield*) together at this time were, like all of the Royal Navy's destroyers and frigates, designed to meet a number of Cold War contingencies. Our main role was to counter the threat posed by Soviet aircraft heading south over the North Atlantic with the ships' long-range missile system, Sea Dart. This we rehearsed both at sea and ashore in simulators, and Sea Dart performed best when intercepting aircraft flying high and with the missile's detection and guidance radar looking over the sea, unhindered by any land mass. *Coventry* was practised in operating in the wild seas of the Atlantic or in the North Sea with both air support and early warning of any threat from the air. Early warning was usually provided by either shore-based maritime patrol aircraft such as Nimrod or the Navy's own carrier-borne aircraft.

Coventry, like her sister ships, was equipped for anti-submarine warfare as well: she carried a Lynx helicopter which could be fitted with homing torpedoes capable of attacking submerged submarines at some distance. Additionally, the ship had torpedo tubes fitted on deck to counter any closer submarine threats. The Lynx was also capable of firing the new Sea Skua missile designed to attack surface targets, though this had yet to be fully evaluated and we had not had the opportunity to practise with it. *Coventry*'s fully automated 4.5-inch gun could be used against air and surface targets up to medium ranges, and for shore bombardment.

In short, we had a bit of everything to throw at an enemy but we would always be at our best with support from other units to provide early warning of any threat, whether from the air, the surface or under the surface. All ships were equipped with electronic listening devices for detecting enemy radar and communication emissions; such intelligence gathering was vital if we were to have advanced warning of enemy activity. If there was an Achilles heel in *Coventry*'s armoury, it was the lack of effective close-in weapons providing a last layer of defence, particularly against air attack. We only had two single 20-mm Oerlikon guns of Second World War vintage, one each side of the bridge.

Coventry was the fifth Royal Navy ship of that name. She had been launched in 1978 by Lady Lewin, the wife of the then First Sea Lord, who always kept in touch with the ship and had come on board for a visit not long before we sailed for Gibraltar. Unfortunately, none of *Coventry*'s predecessors had survived the wars in which they fought. Her immediate predecessor, a light anti-aircraft cruiser, had distinguished herself before being sunk by bomber aircraft in the Mediterranean in 1942, while earlier ships of the name had succumbed to the French or Spanish in one way or another. But we did not dwell much, if at all, on these less encouraging aspects of the ship's history. Our close links with the city of Coventry and the mere fact that the name *Coventry* was associated with a fine fighting record were more than enough to give us something to be proud of and a tradition to preserve. In fact, my godfather Admiral Sir Horace Law had been the gunnery officer of the *Coventry* in 1942 and a member of the *Coventry* Old Hands Association, whose members still meet annually at Coventry Cathedral to remember their lost comrades. There is a memorial to the ship in the crypt of the cathedral: my *Coventry* was later to be commemorated by a new memorial, next to the old one, and members of my ship's company have now also joined the Association.

As it was, we left Gibraltar on 29 March 1982 for a few days of missile firings; we would then return to Portsmouth for some welcome leave and ship maintenance. However, we began to glean from various signals to the Commander-in-Chief of the Fleet, Admiral Sir John Fieldhouse, who was at sea with us, that a change of plan was in the air and that we might not be returning home as planned. It was all something of a mystery. The exercises continued, although we learnt that Sir John had flown home to his headquarters at Northwood. Then, on 2 April, we heard the startling news that South Georgia and the Falkland Islands had been invaded by Argentina and we were instructed to proceed south immediately and at best speed for Ascension Island. This small outcrop of volcanic rock in the South Atlantic is a British dependent territory just south of the Equator with an area of thirty-five square miles. Importantly, Ascension has an air base with a 10,000-foot runway which is leased to the United States, and it was subsequently to become an invaluable halfway staging post, anchorage, refuelling depot and transit camp.

Coventry at this time was in company with HM ships *Antrim*, the flagship, *Glamorgan*, *Sheffield*, *Glasgow*, *Plymouth*, *Yarmouth*, *Brilliant* and *Arrow* together with an accompanying Royal Fleet Auxiliary (RFA) tanker, *Appleleaf*. The large destroyers, *Antrim* and *Glamorgan*, were primarily designed for the anti-surface role, each having four Exocet missile launchers and a twin 4.5-inch gun; but they also had Sea Slug and Sea Cat anti-air missiles, the forerunners of Sea Dart and Sea Wolf, and now virtually obsolete. Their Wessex helicopters were designed for anti-submarine warfare. The frigates in the group, *Plymouth*, *Yarmouth*, *Brilliant* and *Arrow*, were equipped mainly for both anti-submarine and anti-surface work. *Brilliant* and *Arrow*, being comparatively new, were fitted with Exocet and carried Lynx helicopters; *Brilliant* had the short-range anti-air missile Sea Wolf as well.

There were other ships in the area but they were ordered to return to England. Events were unfolding fast and our mission was now becoming a little less confused. Thoughts immediately turned to home and the effects on our families as clearly we were not now going to be back as planned on 6 April. D was in Petersfield, looking after our two daughters Miranda and Alice, then aged nine and six. I consoled myself to think that she was far from being the only one in this part of Hampshire in a similar situation. There were many other families living nearby with sons and husbands in *Coventry*, and in other ships which were based at Portsmouth. I had to banish thoughts of home and concentrate on my job. The captain could not be seen by his sailors to be moping.

When would we be back and what, meanwhile, were we going to be doing? No one was quite sure, but we could soon begin to guess. In any event, I was glad to be in company with some good ships whose commanding officers I knew and liked. I also knew Sandy Woodward quite well as he had been my boss for some time before and I had done business with his staff officers, some of whom I knew very well indeed. How fortunate, then, that we were to be with each other at this time and that we had operated at sea together before. There is a great strength to be gained when working with familiar ships, and the moral and professional support available in such a close-knit task group is invaluable. Furthermore, I knew from the successful weapons training we had just completed that I had a missile system which worked and, more importantly, a tried, tested and confident ship's company of high quality. This was all very reassuring, yet the fact remained that none of us had actually been tested in war, and nor, for that matter, had any of the commanding officers in the Royal Navy at the time. A very few had been involved in putting out colonial bush fires or other such low-intensity campaigns, but that was the sum total of their experience of war.

Tradition acquires a new meaning when you are thrown into the spotlight and involved in momentous events. You become acutely aware that the reputation of both the Navy and your ship is at stake. And so the fighting tradition of the Navy sets a huge challenge for every new generation: it simply must be upheld, and this is what spurs you on. No one wants to fail or to let the side down, and nothing short of performing to the highest standards will do. The Royal Navy, after all, is accustomed to winning, regardless of the odds – and what is more, the country expects as much.

So we headed south, preparing ourselves and our weapons for any eventuality. It was a time of introspection for everyone on board, just as it was also a time for me to rally my ship's company of twenty-eight officers and 271 ratings to the cause. I reflected on my few brushes with war in my early days in the Navy – although this present conflict, if it came to it, looked much more dangerous. I had been serving in the frigate *Eastbourne* as a sub-lieutenant when we steamed all the way at high speed from the Far East to the Persian Gulf during the Kuwait crisis of 1961. This was when the aggressive dictator of

Iraq, General Kassem, threatened to invade Kuwait. By the time we arrived, the crisis had been speedily dealt with and was virtually at an end – much to our disappointment. In those days we had an amphibious squadron based in the Gulf which, with the help of the commando carrier *Bulwark*, landed the Royal Marines on the Kuwait beaches and forestalled the invasion. The excitement was over.

Later, in 1964, when I was the second-in-command of the coastal minesweeper *Lanton*, I had been involved in the confrontation with President Sukarno of Indonesia who was then threatening British North Borneo. Based at Tawau in the traditional gunboat role, we operated in the jungle rivers of Borneo, supporting the Gurkhas and Royal Marines who were fighting in the jungle against the marauding Indonesians. The fighting ashore was fierce at times and the commanding officer of the Gurkhas, Chris Hadow, was killed. I had been with him in his jungle base not long before to learn how the soldiers operated and how best we could support them. Keeping them supplied with cans of beer was, naturally, one of our more important duties.

In the early days, before the shooting war really started, we were ordered to anchor the ship in an open stretch of water and on the median line which marked Indonesian territory on one side and British on the other. The idea was to demonstrate to the Indonesians not far away on the opposite shore that we were intent on defending what was ours. Without warning, however, their shore batteries opened fire on the ship and we began to be hit near the stern. It takes time to haul in the cable and get the anchor up and so I went forward to supervise the breaking of the cable in order to leave the anchor, with a short length of cable, on the sea bed: this was the quickest way of getting the ship moving and out of range of the Indonesian guns. Meanwhile, we fired back with our 40-mm Bofors gun and silenced the enemy. Unfortunately, there was no time to attach a buoy to the end of the anchor cable before we let it go over the side. We got away unharmed and with no casualties – but with only one anchor remaining.

Questions were asked by the authorities back in the UK why *Lanton* had opened fire on the enemy, as the rules laid down by our political masters at that time did not allow it. The case made on our behalf – that we acted in self-defence – was reluctantly accepted, and from then on the rules changed and the war started in earnest. For years afterwards, though, I was pursued by letters from civil servants asking me what I had done with one of *Lanton*'s anchors and accusing me of being thoroughly careless. I was the person, after all, who signed for such equipment when I took up the appointment in the ship and so was held responsible. I suppose I might even have been made to pay for the anchor, which, being made of non-magnetic phosphor-bronze, was a rather expensive item. Fortunately, I never was.

Hauling myself back to the present, I could reflect on the cause of the rapidly deteriorating current situation, which largely arose from a simple failure of deterrence. In 1981, it had been decided that the twenty-five-year-old Antarctic patrol ship *Endurance* would be decommissioned at the end of her tour in March and not be replaced. At the same time, following a government review of defence spending, the Defence Secretary had announced cuts in the number of ships. Some were to be sold to other navies, including, ironically, those that were to prove themselves crucial to operations in the South Atlantic — for example, the aircraft carrier *Invincible*. Other factors were the closing of the British survey base in South Georgia, the denial of full British citizenship to the Falkland Islanders and a decision not to upgrade the Islands' main runway.

All this had sent a strong signal to Argentina that the UK was no longer particularly interested in the Falklands and would not have the resolve to defend them. The Argentinians, who had long held to the belief that the Islands were rightfully theirs, seized the opportunity of taking and, so they hoped, retaining possession of them. The world no doubt thought that the last post had been sounded over yet another far-flung corner of the British Empire. But the world was wrong.

CHAPTER 2

PREPARING
FOR WAR

Just before we turned south, we received a signal instructing all the ships in our group to pair up with those returning to England and obtain any stores from them that might be useful. We were paired off with *Aurora*, an anti-submarine frigate commanded by Commander Tony Wilks. A few hours were spent steaming close alongside her, with a thirty-foot gap between us, while we transferred various spares and essential stores by jackstay, a taut line connecting the two ships with a pulley system to which loads were attached and hauled across by hand. *Aurora* was a completely different class of ship to us, carried dissimilar weapon systems and was powered by steam rather than gas turbine. So there was not much she had in the way of spare parts that were compatible with *Coventry*. But we robbed the ship of all kinds of victuals and food that we knew would be needed for any prolonged time at sea. This manoeuvre was an inspired piece of planning and the first of the many displays of initiative and opportunism throughout the Task Force which were so vital in keeping us fighting fit and the enemy at bay.

The ships were a hive of activity and the sky was almost black with helicopters transferring stores. Many fond farewells were exchanged with friends across the narrow gaps between the ships before we turned away towards the unknown. It felt like a lifeline was being broken as we watched the ships going home until they disappeared over the horizon: they were the last link with a safer world. The happy and carefree weekend in Gibraltar already seemed a distant memory. I remembered that I had sat in the sun in the centre of the Old Town the day before sailing while I wrote a cheerful postcard to D and the girls. At least, I thought now, they will have had some recent news from me.

I had, in fact, managed to scribble a hasty letter to D which I transferred to *Aurora* for posting when she got back to the UK: 'We are off southwards because of the Falkland Island situation – a large group of us. I feel very sad not to be seeing you on 6 April. This is where you have to be a long-suffering and patient naval wife. Shall always be thinking of you and the girls very much. Keep writing because we may be able to get some mail.' I also enclosed a letter to Miranda and Alice: 'Mummy will have told you that my ship will not be back for a few weeks yet. I hope you will always help Mummy when I am not there because she has to do a lot more work without me there. Please write to me often as I always long to hear how you are.'

Our rendezvous with *Aurora* had not only provided us with a multitude of food and stores but had also enabled me to solve a potentially difficult personnel problem. I had five sailors on board who had family concerns back home or important events planned: one, for example, was due to get married and all the arrangements had been made. I was very aware that these men and their families would be very upset if they could not get back to the UK and that their work on board might suffer as a result. Above all, I wanted a contented ship's company. The men could, of course, return home in *Aurora*, but only if I could trade them in for sailors with the same rate and qualifications who would transfer to *Coventry*.

Remarkably, *Aurora* produced five enthusiastic volunteers to sail with us who exactly matched the skills of the sailors who would go home. I fervently hoped they would be happy in *Coventry* and pull their weight. Much later, after the war had ended, Tony Wilks, *Aurora*'s captain, wrote to me: 'Just a note to say a very sincere welcome home to you. You have been much in our prayers and thoughts since that long-ago day of storing off Gib. I hope those members of *Aurora* did you proud and in due course I hope we shall be able to welcome them back on board again.' They certainly did me proud, but sadly they did not all survive.

At this stage, *Coventry* was far from ready for war: we needed ammunition and a number of vital spare parts for machinery, weapon systems and radars. But all this would have to wait until later as we had to speed south in company with the flagship *Antrim* and the rest of the group. So instead we worked hard and kept up our weapons training. As there was no carrier with us yet to provide aircraft to help us practise our main role of air defence, most of our exercises had to be geared to countering surface threats.

Indeed, we believed that the Argentinian Navy, with a number of ships armed with Exocet missiles, might be brave enough to leave their bases to intercept us and confront us on the way down. There was also their carrier, *Veinticinco de Mayo*, named after their national independence day of 25 May. She was the former British carrier *Venerable*, completed in 1945 but extensively modernized since, and could pose a very significant threat with her Skyhawk aircraft embarked. We and the two other Type 42 destroyers frequently practised forming up as a surface-attack group and resolutely rehearsed the appropriate manoeuvres and procedures day and night. In this role we could use our Sea Dart missiles to attack surface targets, and we became a well-drilled and an effective trio.

There was obviously a vast amount of activity and intelligence gathering going on at Commander-in-Chief's Headquarters, the Ministry of Defence, Her Majesty's Dockyards and in many government departments. In fact, we were bombarded with signals providing all kinds of detailed information about the Argentinians and their military strength as well as about our own assembling of troops, ships and support vessels of all kinds. The warfare learning curve was extremely steep and, I thought, somewhat alarming – mainly because of what we might be asked to do.

I wrote to D on 4 April, trusting that there would still be an opportunity for letters to be transferred to a home-going ship: 'I am always hoping and praying that you are well and cheerful but realise it must be rather difficult at the moment. You will be listening to the news and wondering where I am and what I'm doing. What a substitute for a happy return on 6 April. I am very well and in good spirits, though you can imagine I have a fearful responsibility. It's very peaceful here as we steam south to Ascension Island where we wait for the rest of the ships from the UK. So there's a long time yet before anything will happen and hopefully by then there will be a peaceful solution. I think of you always and wish I could be at home with you to help with the children etc. But there we are – after twenty-three years in the Navy, a crisis has finally caught up with me. It has been quite a shock to us all that we had to turn south rather than return to Portsmouth. I imagine I shall be away for about two months, and I think it's best to plan along those lines. We are able to listen to the BBC World Service so we are well up to date with the news from home.'

While the weather remained good, we tried to ensure we still enjoyed some moments of relaxation, however brief, to keep our spirits up. I had a number of the officers to supper in my cabin, an occasion I much enjoyed: it was an opportunity for us to get to know one another better and I think it refreshed us all. Two young lieutenants, Peter Holt and Rodney Heath, both weapons engineers, caused much merriment with their wit and banter. They were very close friends, but one was, sadly, not to return home. On another evening, I was asked to join the officers in the wardroom for dinner by the first lieutenant, who is president of the mess. A captain can expect such an invitation from time to time, and in this instance it was a real pleasure, not least for the entertainment improvised afterwards by some of the officers.

I have always been amazed at the talent to amuse that emerges from among a ship's company, and at their capacity to display it given the slightest opportunity. A sort of 'night out' was organized in the cleared space of the main dining room. Uniforms were dispensed with and beers provided. Skirts, wigs and all kinds of fancy dress materialized from nowhere and Mr Gerry Gilbert, the master-at-arms and the most senior rating responsible for order and discipline on board, caused no little surprise and amusement dressed as a female figure of fun. It was a welcome break in our routine, and a chance for people to unwind and forget their worries, at least for a short while.

The captain of a Royal Navy warship has his own cabin within easy reach of the bridge and operations room, and lives separately from the officers. The officers' cabins and the officers' mess (the wardroom) are often a deck below the captain's quarters. This may seem a curious arrangement, but when you are all together in the close confines of a ship, there are times when a captain needs to be on his own to enjoy a quiet moment or two and mull over the decisions or difficulties of the day. Furthermore, because he is set apart from the officers and the men, a captain is more easily and impartially able to administer the discipline of the ship's company: he is readily accepted as the final arbiter of justice. It is a well-tried and centuries-old system which still works well today. Yet it is not lonely for a captain to live on his own at sea. He is close to many of his officers and men when on the bridge or in the operations room and also when he walks around the ship between decks to talk to his people at work, which would be his custom.

The captain's quarters on 01 deck consist of a day cabin which has space for a desk, a small dining-room table and seating area. Adjoining the day cabin is a bathroom and next door is a bunk space with fitted cupboards, drawers and wardrobe. The area is all on the same level and modest but comfortable. It is self-contained but not isolated: the main entrance to the day cabin leads off a central lobby which provides easy access for anyone who wishes to knock on the captain's door. The captain has two-way communications to the bridge and operations room; a handy microphone enables him to talk to the officers on watch there from anywhere in the day cabin or from the bunk. A door leads off the sleeping quarters almost directly to the foot of the ladder to the bridge; the captain can therefore get to the bridge in a few seconds if called in a crisis. The same short route takes him to ladders down two decks to the operations room.

If anything happens to the captain, the first lieutenant, the second-in-command and an experienced lieutenant-commander, takes over, as he does routinely at sea for short spells when the captain leaves the ship for any reason – briefings aboard the flagship, for example – or if he is in need of some undisturbed rest. In addition to the captain and first lieutenant, in *Coventry* there were twenty-seven other officers, all specialists of some kind or other, except for four who were either sub-lieutenants or midshipmen under training in their first ship after completing their initial training ashore. The largest category among these officers were of the seaman specialization, which meant they could aspire to command ships. Apart from the captain, the first lieutenant was the most senior of them on board. The others included four warfare officers, the navigating and communications officers, flight commander, pilot and two fighter controllers. There were three other more junior seamen officers, all qualified officers-of-the-watch, whose job it was to keep watch on the bridge and control the movement of the ship, day and night, under the navigating officer's eagle eye. (All the orders to the quartermaster – or helmsman – to alter the course and speed of the ship are given either by the captain or officer-of-the-watch on the bridge.)

In *Coventry*, the seaman officers managed the operations department, which consisted of seaman ratings of many specializations trained to operate missiles, guns, torpedoes, sonars and radars. They were also trained to conduct various evolutions such as berthing, anchoring, replenishing fuel and ammunition at sea and the use of boats. Additionally, seamen could carry out bridge watch-keeping duties as quartermasters, bosun's mates and lookouts under the supervision of officers-of-the-watch. The weapons engineer officer and his deputy led the largest department of technical experts in the ship, maintaining and repairing all the vital weapons, sensors and power supplies. The marine engineers were also a large team of skilled ratings presided over by the marine engineer officer and a deputy. They looked after all the complex machinery of the main propulsion units and provided much of the expertise in damage control and fire-fighting. Not least was the supply officer, who managed all the victuals and stores in the ship as well as being trained as the flight deck officer, controlling the movements and safety of the helicopter. There was also a young supply officer who acted as the captain's secretary: in *Coventry*, he found himself qualifying as an assistant flight deck officer to help cope with the intensive flying operations.

All these departments were structured so as to ensure the ship was properly run and fought. The chief petty officers were the most senior ratings, with petty officers, then leading, able, ordinary and junior rates below them. The ship's ratings were divided into 'divisions' in the care of a divisional officer, normally of the same specialist background, who looked after their welfare and monitored their performance. Every rating, therefore, had an officer whom he could approach and talk to freely whenever he wanted. This was a well-proven system and one which helped to maintain a content and efficient ship's company. It ensured that any personal grievances or problems were quickly heard and dealt with before they got any worse.

Furthermore it meant that the captain would be spared any deputations from unhappy sailors appearing at his door.

The design of a warship is, of course, complex, having to balance the requirements for a reasonable living standard on board with the need to pack in as many weapon systems as possible in not too large or cumbersome a hull. While the Russian Navy in the Cold War era built impressive-looking ships bristling with weapons and radar antennae, the cramped and uncomfortable spaces left for the crews would not have enhanced either their motivation or their fighting effectiveness. In this respect, the Type 42 is better designed, packing a good punch with its weapons at the same time as providing some measure of comfort for both officers and men. Moreover, the Royal Navy's ships are generally much better at operating in rough weather than their Russian counterparts, whose heavily loaded upper decks, superstructures and masts make them poor sea-keepers in these conditions.

The physical confines of a ship where a comparatively large number of people live closely together necessarily demand a tight organization to ensure that every individual knows exactly what his responsibilities are and that he works with others without conflict or confusion. In *Coventry* each department had its own office run by a senior rating who was responsible for manning all the positions around the ship required to be filled by specialists from that department. The first lieutenant had overall responsibility for the manning of the ship in all situations, whether in action, peacetime cruising, in harbour or for certain evolutions at sea such as the replenishment of fuel. He, too, had a senior rating running a routine or regulating office which produced 'daily orders' informing the whole ship of the requirements of the day and the routine in force. This office provided details of the manning requirements for all departments in every contingency. Here, the name of every sailor would be listed against his precise position in the ship and the duty he was expected to perform there; thus everybody was matched according to his training, skill and experience to the right job, which in turn contributed to the efficient running and fighting of the ship. Whenever the action-station alarm was sounded, for example, there could be no time for questions or people getting lost: in about two minutes, everyone had to be in their correct positions, ready to fight, wearing anti-flash hood and gloves and carrying lifejacket, gas mask and survival suit. And that's how it was in *Coventry*, for weeks on end.

As we headed south to the Equator, the choppy grey-green seas gave way to a brilliant blue calm, and as the temperature rose, dolphins could be seen riding the pressure waves close to the bows of the ship. They would glide, twist and turn at speed underwater, playing like children, and occasionally leap gracefully out of the water, as if showing off. They became friends, staying with the ship for hours on end and providing absorbing entertainment. In the tropics, the thin white clouds melted away to reveal a clear blue sky, and in the warmer water silver-blue flying fish propelled themselves out of the sea ahead to glide on their wings before darting down again. The silence as the ship sliced through the peaceful sea was broken only by the splashing of the bow wave against the hull, the low hum of machinery and the throb of the propellers. We sometimes had to remind ourselves that we were in a warship rather than a cruise liner. It was, of course, the calm before the storm, and this is exactly how it felt.

My letter home of 9 April, which would reach the UK via Ascension Island, expressed the hope for a peaceful outcome to the dispute with Argentina; it then dwelt mostly on domestic practicalities. I briefed D on paying the utility bills, having the gas boiler serviced and all the other things I usually dealt with; I even went into some detail about maintaining the correct pressures on the tyres of the car. It must have been a very dull letter, but I evidently thought it was necessary at the time, and no doubt I felt better for sending it. 'Here I am,' I wrote, 'still steaming south. It's very hot. We're all praying for a political solution and a quick end to the problem – otherwise we could be here for several months. That would be ghastly, but I suppose you and I must prepare ourselves for the worst case and maybe I will not be back till about August. Hardly bears thinking about. P.S. Just got your telegram – fabulous! Now I know you're alive and well. It's quite cheered me up.'

We arrived off Ascension on 11 April. It was certainly a relief to be looking at a friendly shoreline again as we dug out white uniforms and bared our lily-white limbs to the sun. But there was little time for relaxation. General preparation and weapons training continued and intensified. Ascension became a frantically busy forward operating base from where we took on a vast amount of stores and spares by helicopter. Not least, we received charts of the Falklands – which was just as well, since for most of us they had been no more than distant dots on the atlas at school.

I continued to be impressed with the mass of intelligence and briefing material on the Argentinian forces that was being made available to us. There seemed to be nothing we did not know about them: there were even assessments of the key players from

President Galtieri downwards, their strengths and weaknesses. It was not encouraging, however, to count up the number of front-line aircraft available to them – 200 or more – and to read the brief on their Navy. Its two German-built 209-class diesel submarines were modern and armed with very effective homing torpedoes; they would be a nasty threat if properly deployed. We had, on first reckoning at least, every reason to be worried.

Such anxieties were brought home even more as we carried out frequent first-aid and damage-control exercises, simulating fire and flooding. And as we secured the ship for action – this time for real – by removing all the trappings and comforts of peacetime it made everything below decks look distinctly stark; this had a particularly sobering effect on the ship's company. Unwanted items which might add to the fire risk or impede movement around the ship had to be thrown over the side, and these included wind-surfing boards and even a sailing dinghy. This was a new experience for us all.

We spent three or four days off Ascension acquiring as many stores and spares and as much extra equipment as we could. It was a useful breathing space, giving the Lynx helicopter crew time to familiarize themselves with the loading and firing of the new Sea Skua missiles which had been flown down to Ascension and then transferred by helicopter to us and to other ships. We also took the opportunity to mount machine guns in the helicopter to convert it into some sort of gunship. A certain amount of ingenuity was required to make rotating platforms for the guns, and these were eventually fabricated from the steel swivel legs of office chairs.

Further preparations for war included painting a large Union Jack on the bridge roof to make it easier for our aircraft to identify us as friendly. The Type 42s were instructed to paint a thick black stripe down both sides of the ship abreast the funnel, a measure designed to assist our submariners in target recognition – and we certainly did not wish to be blown out of the water by a British torpedo. (This was a very reasonable precaution, for the Argentinians also had Type 42 destroyers, two to be precise, one built in the UK and the other in South America, and their crews had been trained by the Royal Navy.) Our pennant number, D118, carried on either side below the bridge, was painted over to make identification more difficult for the enemy, and with dark grey paint we toned down all the white-painted areas and bright fittings on the upper deck to make us stand out less against the horizon. In short, nothing was left to chance and every effort was made to secure an advantage over the enemy.

We were still off Ascension on 13 April when I sent a letter off to D: 'It's very agonizing listening to the news and hearing the lack of progress in the [diplomatic] talks. So we move closer to fighting which I think could be a disaster for UK as well as for the RN. Our task will not be easy and it's likely to be a long drawn-out affair. I doubt whether Margaret Thatcher and her government would survive if this happened. Meanwhile we exercise and prepare the ship for war – which is traumatic in itself. The ship is painted in its war colours. Quite a sight. I am determined to enter Portsmouth harbour the way the ship looks now – it would cause quite a stir! The loneliness of command, especially in difficult times, is quite a strain – though I know I shall cope all right. I am in very good health, which is a blessing, and remain outwardly cheerful, but inwardly anxious. I long to get back and miss you a lot.' I added a PS: 'While I remember, there are two envelopes in the drawers of my desk addressed to you. They tell you how much money you get if I fail to return from the war. Thought I had better mention it! At least you won't be short of cash.'

Meanwhile, our intelligence had also informed us that the Argentinians possessed the latest French Super Étendard strike aircraft fitted with Exocet anti-ship missiles. These were designed to be flown from carriers, but the *Veinticinco de Mayo* was not yet properly equipped to take them. Manned by naval personnel, whose pilots and engineers had been trained by the French, the aircraft now flew from shore bases in southern Argentina, mainly from Rio Grande, the closest airfield to the Falkland Islands and the likely operating area of the Carrier Battle Group. (French engineers were, it was rumoured, still assisting the Argentinians at these bases during the conflict.) Argentina had many other aircraft, mainly the American Skyhawk, Israeli Dagger and French Mirage. The first two carried 500- or 1,000-pound bombs and the latter radar-homing missiles; all had built-in cannons, either 20-mm or 30-mm. A number of nations, some of them our allies, would be looking on with keen interest to see how their weapon systems performed in a real war.

Just before leaving Ascension, I had a final opportunity to send mail to the UK and so wrote another letter to D in reply to hers of 9 April. In it I remarked: 'This operation is going to be difficult and the predicted strong winds and cold weather will make it all a bit of an endurance test. But I feel sure I shall survive all right – I'm quite used to rough weather. I am very confident, too, that the ship will do everything well and that before you know where you are, I shall be gliding past the round tower into Portsmouth harbour.'

The Admiral, Sandy Woodward, had by this time transferred his flag to *Glamorgan*, whose captain was Mike Barrow, and before we left Ascension he invited all the commanding officers of the small 'spearhead' force to a briefing on board to share his thoughts on what might lie ahead and how we might conduct operations. It was the first time we had all met face to face in this new situation and were able to share our concerns and to hear answers to our many questions. After the Admiral's staff had put forward some initial plans for action, there was an open discussion and exchange of ideas about what might be required of us. The potential for a prolonged air battle was central to much of the deliberations. We were far outnumbered in the air and no landing of troops to recapture the Islands could possibly take place before the air threat was largely eliminated.

I had known Mike Barrow for some time and met him first when I worked with him in the early 1970s at Britannia Royal Naval College, Dartmouth, where I was a member of the training staff and he was the commander. He lived near me in Petersfield, as did some of his officers in *Glamorgan* whom I also knew well. I was to see *Glamorgan* from time to time, mostly though my binoculars, during the conflict. She played a prominent part in the war from the very beginning, distinguishing herself particularly in shore bombardment as she softened up the enemy on the Islands; she fired thousands of rounds of 4.5-inch shells until her gun barrels were nearly worn out. Mike was a very experienced commanding officer – a true sea dog who knew how to fight a ship and get the best out of his men. Towards the very end of the war, *Glamorgan* was most unlucky to be hit by an Exocet missile launched from the shore some twenty miles away, which caused severe damage and killed thirteen of her crew. Despite this, the ship eventually got home safely.

The tasks before us were formidable and the Type 42 destroyers were clearly going to have to play a key part. None the less, I think we all felt better for the meeting, seeing old friends again and finding out more about what lay ahead, but there was still not a great deal to be encouraged or confident about. We bid our farewells and Sandy Woodward escorted us to the ladders from which the boats would leave and speed us back to our ships. He wished us all good luck.

As a former submariner, Sandy Woodward must have wondered whether a more senior and experienced sea-going admiral would be sent down to command the Carrier Battle Group in his place; it would not have been at all surprising. I had no thoughts along these lines at the time, though I heard talk of it later. There were two obvious candidates, both of whom had commanded the Third Flotilla consisting of carriers and an amphibious group – an ideal qualification. However, it made sense to leave Sandy Woodward in charge: he was the man on the spot and he knew a large number of the ships and commanding officers. A change in command could have been disruptive. The captain of *Hermes*, Captain Linley Middleton, was an experienced aviator and Captain Jeremy Black of *Invincible* was probably the most experienced and wisest of commanding officers in the Navy at that time. As it was, I was always encouraged to hear Sandy Woodward listen to the views and advice of Jeremy Black when he faced difficult decisions. I could hear these conversations from time to time on the command communication circuits. He was never too proud to hear what other wise heads had to say.

I was now able to brief my warfare officers more fully and inform the ship's company as a whole of the likely operations required of us. The latter was not an easy job as I had to balance encouragement against the seriousness of the threat and the considerable risks. The Admiral came on board himself a few days later by helicopter, as he did to the other ships in our group, to speak to the ship's company and tell them how he saw events unfolding. He spoke sternly and realistically about the very difficult tasks facing us and left us in no doubt as to the dangers ahead. It was the first time we heard someone say that war was possible and that we could expect ship losses and casualties on our side. This came as a shock to many on board but it was the right line to take and I think it actually helped us to concentrate even more on preparing for what was clearly going to be a tough fight.

I had a good discussion with the Admiral in my cabin. I felt he knew me and the ship well as he had been on board before. This made it easier for me to air my anxieties privately and to discuss how the war might go. It was a very valuable few minutes during which we could not even sit down as the decks had been cleared of carpets and all the furniture in the cabin stored for action. I commented on the size of his staff and asked whether it was sufficient in numbers and expertise to support him if we embarked on a war. He agreed with the point I was making and I observed later how two senior captains, one a submarine specialist and the other an aviator (whose name I had suggested), had been flown out from the UK to join his staff. Again, this was reassuring.

Sandy Woodward was not a man of obvious charm or warmth on first meeting, but you soon noticed his genuine concern for those who worked for him and his interest in them. He exuded competence, and he had a mathematical mind which evaluated every situation carefully and analytically. Decisions would always be soundly based and no doubt arrived at only after a few graphs or flowcharts had been drawn. His background could not have been more appropriate to the task which now faced him, for he had been brought up in the post-war era of nuclear engineering and advanced computer systems, and he possessed an intimate knowledge of anti-submarine warfare. I liked him, had complete faith in him and did not mind his tough approach, but I know that others took longer to respond to him and to appreciate his rather complex character. He certainly could be forceful and did not suffer fools gladly. But there was no doubt that his was a very safe pair of hands and he would do nothing hastily or on a whim. He also clearly enjoyed the confidence of his superiors at home, particularly the Commander-in-Chief of the Fleet, who was also a submariner and must have known him well.

Before Sandy Woodward left *Coventry*, he admired the pictures on my cabin walls – or bulkheads, as they are called in the Navy – and one in particular painted by my mother of the Cuillin hills on the Isle of Skye which he seemed to like. Having operated out of Faslane, he must have known that skyline well. I said he could have the picture if we won the war. This was meant quite seriously and he accepted the offer in the same vein. Two other pictures in my cabin had been painted by my artist uncle; another was a peaceful watercolour river scene I had collected. But this was not the time, unfortunately, to discuss such things, so I escorted him to the flight deck and watched him fly off. He had now joined *Hermes*, which would remain his

Coventry passes under the Forth Bridge on her way to Rosyth dockyard, October 1981
(Crown Copyright / MOD)

Turning south for the Falklands, 2 April 1982 *(Crown Copyright / MOD)*

David Hart Dyke as a
midshipman *(David Hart Dyke)*

The engagement
photograph of his wife,
D, the author kept in
his cabin *(David Hart Dyke)*

Postmark made by a member of *Coventry*'s company to stamp on letters home
(David Hart Dyke)

Darling Miranda & Alice
I miss you very much and long to see you again. Thank you for your lovely letters. Here's a picture of my ship firing a missile at an aeroplane and my helicopter

firing a missile at a patrol boat. Good picture isn't it ?! Please look after Mummy won't you and tell her not to worry about me. Lots of love Daddy xxxxx ooooo

A letter and drawing sent by the author to his children on 11 May 1982 *(David Hart Dyke)*

A Wessex helicopter winches up the author from *Coventry* for a briefing on the flagship, mid-April 1982 *(David Hart Dyke)*

Four of the indispensable Sea Harriers and Harrier GR 3s on the flight deck of HMS *Hermes* *(Imperial War Museum FKD 2,343)*

flagship throughout his time in the South Atlantic. I was not to see him again until we were both back in England.

On 15 April, the main force of ships from UK, comprising the Carrier Battle Group with the carriers *Hermes* and *Invincible*, had joined us, although they remained just over the horizon and out of sight as we were ordered to continue southwards. The plan was to proceed to a holding position, some 1,000 miles north of the Falkland Islands and the same distance from South Georgia, and to prepare for whatever the authorities at home might want us to do. The hope was that the Argentinians would think that the Battle Group was still off Ascension Island, which indeed it was, but they would not know that a smaller force under the command of Captain John Coward in *Brilliant* was quite close to the Falkland Islands and ready to take any action necessary. The aim, therefore, was to preserve an element of surprise.

We were now a little clearer in our purpose and in company with *Brilliant*, *Sheffield*, *Glasgow*, *Arrow* and RFA *Appleleaf*. *Antrim* (Captain Brian Young) and *Plymouth* (Captain David Pentreath) did not continue with us as they were to be detached and sent to South Georgia together with RFA *Tidespring*, to supply their fuel, and RFA *Fort Austin*. The latter, normally unarmed, had embarked special forces and Lynx helicopters with Sea Skua missiles for operations to retake South Georgia.

I watched *Plymouth* set off in the murky weather, her stern dipping down and churning up the rough sea as she accelerated away. These ships had a daunting task ahead of them and I silently wished them good luck as they disappeared into the descending gloom. I must admit that I felt quite relieved that I was not going with them. As it transpired, *Antrim* and *Plymouth* were instrumental, rather against the odds, in recapturing South Georgia amidst fearsome weather conditions. It was a remarkable exploit and a great boost to our morale when we learnt of it.

We maintained complete silence on all our transmissions of radar, sonar and communications in order to remain undetected. At the same time we manoeuvred by light signal and practised surface warfare day and night. Our energetic and imaginative leader, John Coward, developed the idea of capturing an enemy warship with his Royal Marine detachment, whose members would abseil down a rope from his helicopter after it had approached from behind at dead of night. Once on deck, they would go to selected positions, creep silently about like so many James Bonds and take out key personnel in charge of the ship. We thought this might be a useful tactic – such were the uncertainties at the time – and it was duly practised against my ship. I alone had prior warning and the marines got on board all right, but we caught them before they were able to do any harm.

I must admit I found this a difficult time, although it was only in my letters home that I revealed my anxieties. It seemed very hard on D that I should share with her all my weaknesses and concerns when I ought instead to have been doing my best to boost her own morale, but this was my only outlet for expressing how I really felt. My letter writing also did much to help me clear my mind and put my worries about the family to one side. Each letter I wrote was, I suppose, an attempt to get a last message home whenever the opportunity presented itself. I could then direct my thoughts solely to the ship and my sailors.

CHAPTER 3

TESTING TIMES

As we left the tropics and continued towards more southerly latitudes, the weather began to change. We were back in our blue uniforms and jerseys as the ship bounced around in the mounting seas. It was much like being in the North Atlantic, and when you went on to the upper deck, your face would be stung with salt spray blown in the wind off the cold grey sea. I often found a rough sea and a strong wind exhilarating when blessed with both the power and control of a warship which was able to ride the waves and make light of the buffeting against its hull. It was a question of choosing the right course and speed to tame the effects of the weather and make progress without causing any damage to fittings and equipment on the upper deck. The worst motion occurred when you had to maintain high speed directly into a heavy sea: the ship would rise high over a wave pointing skywards and then slam down hard into a trough with a disturbing shudder, and you prayed that the bow would pull out of the trough before the next wave thundered down on top of it. This violent pitching was always to be avoided, and so you had to alter the course of the ship to put the weather more on the bow rather than right ahead. The ship's stabilizers did little to counter pitching, but they did reduce rolling in a beam sea – although this was more for the benefit of the ship's sensors and weapon systems than any weak stomachs on board.

We could cope with the worsening weather, but for me this period before the conflict started was the most testing, and the most frightening. It was a time of both self-examination and adjustment. Somehow I had to remove from my mind all thoughts of a safe and familiar peacetime world and come to terms with the increasing likelihood of real danger and violence. And I found this far from easy. I remember having a terrible hollow feeling in my stomach as the full realization of what was happening dawned on me. With it came a sense of being trapped, with no possible escape, and of being pushed into a fight of someone else's making – a lottery of life or death. I felt that I was being swept helplessly along in a fast-flowing river to an uncertain end, and that I was unable to strike out for the banks and safety. I was both afraid of being caught up in some- thing I didn't much like and angry that I had been.

These days of not knowing whether we were going to have to fight or not were unnerving, mentally exhausting and, for most people, extremely hard to endure. For my part, I could scarcely believe that we were going to be asked to resolve the issue by force when we were so heavily outnumbered on the ground and in the air: I thought the Argentinian Air Force alone could win the war and that even just the two small 209-class submarines could bring us to our knees by picking off the aircraft carriers or the troop-carrying ships as they approached the landing area.

I feared for both the reputation and the future of the Royal Navy should we fail.

When I was at the Naval Staff College in the mid-1970s, one of my duties had been to run a paper exercise for the students, setting them the task of preventing an imminent Argentinian invasion of the Falkland Islands. This indicates how topical the subject was in the Ministry of Defence at the time, for Staff College students were often given potential problems like this to brainstorm their way through and, with any luck, to solve. The students, split into syndicates, were given realistic information on the British forces available from all three services and the forces opposing them. It was very much a logistical exercise, with all the supporting tankers, stores and ammunition ships included in the data, and the 'operation' was meticulously studied over two or three days. In the end, however, all the syndicates concluded that, with the forces available, it would not be possible to prevent an invasion: the enemy's superiority in numbers and the logistical difficulties of maintaining our forces so far from home for any length of time made it all too risky. These conclusions were, I think, consistent with the generally accepted views of the senior military in London, which would presumably have been made known to government ministers. I found it ironic that I was now being involved in the real thing, and that there were probably even fewer forces available to us than there had been in the paper exercise. I rather wished that the students' conclusions had been more positive.

I imagined the First Sea Lord, Admiral Sir Henry Leach, telling the Prime Minister that of course the Navy could do it. After all, this had been the traditional response of First Sea Lords over the centuries – although in the past the Navy had been much larger and better equipped, and our enemies had generally been weaker. Now I wondered whether the powers that be had even had a chance to assess the threat accurately or to work out how we could sustain a large force 8,000 miles from home before Admiral Leach gave his assurance to Mrs Thatcher. As it was, in his first meeting with the Prime Minister, when the latest intelligence reports indicated that the Falkland Islands were under imminent threat of invasion, Admiral Leach had been asked whether we could really recapture the Islands. 'Yes,' he had said, 'we could, and in my judgement, though it is not my business to say so, we should.' 'Why do you say that?' the Prime Minister had asked. 'Because if we do not,' came the emphatic reply, 'or if we pussyfoot in our actions and do not achieve complete success, in another few months we shall be living in a different country whose words count for little.' The Prime Minister had warmed very much to what she had just heard from her confident First Sea Lord. From that moment, the Navy had been mobilized and the preparations for war on a large scale had begun.

Naturally, I knew none of this at the time. In fact, such were my uncertainties about any military action that, before we left Ascension, I had written a letter to my brother-in-law Richard Luce, who was the Minister of State in the Foreign Office with responsibilities, among others, for the defence of the Falkland Islands. My point, and it was one I made with some seriousness, was that we really had to keep on negotiating, for we would not be able to win any war. It was a feeling shared by some of my colleagues. But by the time Richard received this letter, he had resigned, along with the Foreign Secretary, Lord Carrington: they had both felt it had been the honourable thing to do. Even so, it is possible that my letter may have given rise to newspaper comment to the effect that senior naval officers in the front line were not so confident about the outcome of any military action: it may even have helped to introduce a note of realism into proceedings and perhaps to counter the jingoistic 'Knock 'em for six' talk abounding in the media.

With the benefit of hindsight, I can see how the experience of Admiral Leach, who had been a Flag Officer of Flotillas and Commander-in-Chief of the Fleet before he was appointed First Sea Lord, would have encouraged him to believe that a Royal Navy Task Force and embarked troops could recapture the Islands – even if he had no doubt about the risks involved and the likely loss of ships in the process. He had served in the Second World War and so had seen our island nation galvanized into action and displaying all its remarkable resolve as it fought a desperately hard war, often far from home.

Henry Leach's father had been the captain of the new battleship *Prince of Wales* in December 1941 when she, along with the battlecruiser *Repulse*, was sunk by Japanese bombers off the coast of Malaya. Captain Leach was among the hundreds of sailors lost. His son, then serving in a cruiser based in Singapore, saw his father sail from the base on this last fateful voyage. These two capital ships had been despatched to the Far East following a political directive from the British government, and this despite the considerable Japanese threat and the fact that they lacked any air cover. (The aircraft carrier *Indomitable* was to have been part of the force, but the ship was damaged when she ran aground and no replacement was made available.) Their subsequent loss was a tragic and expensive lesson that even ships which could manoeuvre freely in open waters were vulnerable to air attack and were best protected by ship-borne aircraft immediately at hand. As it happened, no fighter aircraft were available from shore either – until it was too late. Henry Leach himself would have forgotten none of this, and I know that he would have had it in mind when he advised Margaret Thatcher. Protection of our ships against the threat from the air was, as always, going to be a critical factor, and our very limited force of Sea Harriers embarked in *Hermes* and *Invincible*, along with our ships' missiles and guns, was going to have to provide it.

These days were especially hard, I think, because I had to remain outwardly unafraid and cheerful to provide my ship's company with strong leadership. My men began to watch me more closely and listen to every word I uttered: any chink revealed in my armour would have considerably increased their anxiety and even, perhaps, reduced their will to fight. Their lives were in my hands and I could sense that they felt it. As the chances of a political settlement slipped away and war began to seem a real possibility, we became increasingly concerned. A mood of anxiety pervaded the ship.

However, once we were on our way and well south of Ascension, my confidence returned and I found myself more at ease with the situation as I concentrated on lifting everyone's spirits while we prepared vigorously for action. I was even beginning to become slightly impatient: if there was going to be fighting, I just wanted to get on with it. Although I was still not certain we could win a war, I now began to realize there was no option but to fight and to do our utmost to rid the Islands of their occupiers. As I wrote in a letter at this time: 'I am getting more resigned to my circumstances, though it has been quite difficult to adjust and this has left me feeling pretty worn out.

But I am definitely on top of it now and I shall be ready to go when I have to. It is hard work being the figurehead and the one who must remain calm, cheerful and confident – and all those other things you are expected to be as a captain in charge of 300 sailors. So I put a brave face on everything and hope for the best. My sailors are bearing up well and ready for anything, and you can be sure that I and *Coventry* will do our bit.'

For many in the ship, the experience of preparing themselves and *Coventry* for war was traumatic. Will forms had to be completed and last letters home written. Morphine was issued, along with lifejackets, survival suits and identity discs. Pictures, trophies and soft furnishings had to be removed. All this had a dramatic impact. I was personally issued with a lifejacket and other lifesaving equipment by the damage-control petty officer, Michael Fowler, who was held in high regard by everyone, not only in the ship but, we learnt later, by his community at home.

Meanwhile, letters from family and friends and heartfelt messages from home wishing us good luck and a safe return were very welcome, even if they added to the tension and high-lighted the risks ahead. To receive this support, and to know we had that of the country at large, was immensely reassuring. The many telegrams we received were posted on the ship's main notice-board for all to see. Among them was one from the Lord Mayor of Coventry, Councillor Eddie Weaver, who had been on board the ship for a day at sea only a few months earlier.

A rather frightened petty officer came to see me and asked somewhat nervously whether the cross of nails, presented to us by Coventry Cathedral and always displayed in a prominent part of the ship, could be left where it was and not stowed away. I think he felt it was a kind of symbol of hope and survival, as

I expect it was to others as well. I agreed, and so this cross stood conspicuously in its familiar place throughout the conflict. It was made from three large, silver-coated medieval nails which had held together the roof timbers of the fourteenth-century cathedral when it had been so badly bombed in the Second World War. The nails were mounted on a wooden base, and we used to place the cross on a makeshift altar when we held the traditional Sunday morning services at sea.

For my part, I wondered if I should not transfer some of my more valuable belongings to one of our support vessels, which would be less exposed to danger. As we had not expected to be going to war and had also recently been involved in flag-showing duties, I had all the trappings of peacetime entertaining on board – not to mention all my best uniforms for every occasion, as well as my telescope and sword, both of which had belonged to my father and been used by him throughout his career in the Navy. I also had two crested George II candlesticks, a silver salver and, of course, a number of fine watercolours. Everything was stowed in my cabin. I soon discarded the idea, however: it would not do much for morale if my goods and chattels were seen being transferred to another ship.

Besides, there were other, more important matters to deal with. We were now advised to offer the Hong Kong Chinese personnel in our ships the opportunity to leave before hostilities started. These enterprising and industrious people have served the Royal Navy and been loyal to the British Crown for some two hundred years, and we were fortunate to have four of them with us, three laundrymen and a tailor. They are not paid by the Navy and are therefore unofficial employees, but they are offered board and lodging and a licence to trade, and they send most of the profits from their work back to their families. This is their chosen way of life and they put up with considerable hardship at sea, living and working in the smallest of spaces to provide the ship's company with immaculately clean and expertly pressed uniforms. All my Chinese men, even though they were well aware of the risks, chose to stay on board. It was a real show of loyalty and one I greatly valued.

Similarly, the civilian manager of the NAAFI canteen, Ron Fletcher, and his assistant had the option to leave before hostilities began. But they also chose to stay and continued to serve in the shop, providing a welcome selection of sweets – known as 'nutty' in the Navy – and other provisions. (I certainly much appreciated the chocolate bars which helped me keep going when I was stuck on the bridge for long periods.) What is more, they volunteered for specific naval duties when we were in action, which showed remarkable devotion to both the ship and the crew. I believe we had to enrol them formally into the rating structure of the Navy before they were legally permitted to take part in any action, but they went on to become valuable members of the war-fighting team.

By now, we were drawing inexorably closer to the disputed and dangerous waters off the Falklands. The commanding officers in our spearhead group met several times in *Brilliant* to discuss plans and consider the implications of the latest developments: these were invaluable occasions as we could share our views and concerns with friends, and I always came away from them feeling better. We normally transferred to *Brilliant* by helicopter, often in stormy conditions. But flying at wave-top height in heavy, spray-laden seas and landing on the pitching deck of a small ship was not my idea of fun. Worse still was being winched off the deck with just a strop under your arms and on the end of a long cable which wound you up to the helicopter hovering above. As you dangled close to the helicopter's cabin, you were grabbed by a crewman and dumped unceremoniously on the floor of the aircraft. If we did not travel by helicopter, we went in a Sea Rider, a fast and rigid inflatable boat. This method also had its excitements in bad weather. It was all you could do to hang on and keep your backbone intact as you leapt from wave-top to wave-top. One had to be fit.

The last time we met in *Brilliant*, it seemed almost certain that we would soon be at war, and there was a lot to think about. Afterwards, I shared a lift in a helicopter with Sam Salt of *Sheffield*. We were duly bundled into the waiting, whirring machine like two pieces of cargo. The ride was bumpy and noisy, and it was impossible to talk. I got out first and, as I did so, Sam pressed me on the shoulder as a way of saying goodbye and good luck. I wondered whether I would see him again.

I was sorry to say goodbye to *Brilliant*. This was to be both the last time that I would work with her and the last time we operated as a group. I shall always have happy memories of those times with *Brilliant*, *Sheffield*, *Glasgow* and *Arrow*, and of the captains of those ships. John Coward inspired us all with his energy, ideas and determination. He was fearless, and he always kept you on your toes. Much later, on 11 July, when the war had been won, he wrote me a touching letter: 'I am sorry not to have written before, but we are now on our way home with poignant memories of that brave little squadron that set out for the South Atlantic with such determination, and you are so much in our thoughts that I now feel compelled to write. We stopped the ship and mustered in our Number One uniforms in your honour as we followed what seemed to be that familiar track homeward. Same bright sunshine, same bright sea, same wheeling albatross – but no longer you and *Sheffield* creaming alongside to brave it in my sea-boat or hurry across in your Lynx. We sadly miss your graceful ship and your merry company and thank God that so many of you have survived to carry her memory. Rest assured at least that there are others apart from yourselves who remember her with the utmost pride. We were indeed a "happy few" who sailed together, and even though some of our ships are left behind, you have brought our nation great honour.'

But this kindness of John Coward's was far in the future. Soon we would be joining the Carrier Battle Group in the air defence role, and once again, it was important to brief and prepare the ship's company. I spoke frequently to the whole ship on the main broadcast but also conducted more personal briefings with the officers and senior ratings in their messes. Today's officers and sailors, all volunteers, are intelligent, highly skilled and generally well motivated. So I could not gloss over the facts or give them a misleading picture of what we would be up against, but at the same time I wished to be as reassuring as it was possible to be. These were important sessions and I invariably came away from them with the impression that I could rely on the support of a very willing team of professionals.

The pace of events was now accelerating. The weather was becoming very cold and windy, and on occasions the seas were mountainous. The southern ocean between latitudes 40 degrees to 60 degrees south is notoriously rough all the year round, and it provided quite a challenge. On one occasion, I had to refuel alongside a tanker in a full gale. It required a cool head and some skilful steering by the quartermaster to avoid a collision or carrying away the fuelling hose stretched between the ships. I found it easier to control the ship from the wings of the bridge rather than remain inside behind the pelorus compass on the centre line. By the time the replenishment was completed, I was soaked to the skin by the heavy sea thrown up between the two ships – a condition which I noticed caused some amusement among those on watch in the warmth and shelter of the bridge.

I would spend long hours on the bridge, watching the ocean and the many albatross as they glided and wheeled effortlessly over the waves, occasionally stroking the surface with their wing-tips – seemingly with not a care in the world. It was both exhilarating and humbling to be ploughing through these powerful seas in a ship which was a mere speck on the earth's surface and entirely at the mercy of Mother Nature. The sea instils a sense of awe and timelessness. Ships have passed through it and fought over it since the beginning of time, but it remains forever restless and unchanging. It makes us wonder about the purpose of human life, and reminds us that we are only here for the smallest fraction of time. As Psalm 107 has it: 'They that go down to the sea in ships, that do business in great waters; these see the works of the Lord, and his wonders in the deep.'

But this was not the moment to be contemplating the miracle of the universe, the mysteries of our existence or even the futility of war. Set against the vastness of the ocean, *Coventry* was totally insignificant. She was, however, a major warship with 300 souls on board and about to confront a formidable foe. As we neared the Falklands, I scribbled a letter to D on 28 April: 'I don't know when you will get this letter, but you will eventually, I'm sure. All is well here and I am bearing up well as I lead my ship's company into war. What a thing to be doing! But regrettably I have no choice and although I hate it all, I am ready for it. I have terrible thoughts about leaving you and the girls to continue life without me. I do hope if it came to it you will be very, very brave and recover quickly. Life must go on and you three must be happy. So you will try very hard, won't you?... But I will be back, so hold on till then and don't worry about me – I am in good health and the ship is ready for anything.'

I had always been impressed with the British forces' postal organization as I travelled around the globe in ships. Now, even in the South Atlantic, every effort was being made to get mail to and from ships, although clearly this was far from easy. Ascension Island provided the first stop for mail flown from the UK; it could then either be embarked in the many passing ships destined for the Task Force, which would take at least a week, or put in a watertight canister in a long-range RAF patrol aircraft and dropped in the sea near the main force for a ship to recover. Helicopters could then distribute the mail to individual ships as the opportunities arose. Those of us operating near the Islands were obviously the most difficult to reach, and our own letters home could only travel to Ascension by sea.

It was now the end of April and the Carrier Battle Group, with its host of supporting warships and supply vessels, was nearing our position. A 200-mile exclusion zone had been established around the Falkland Islands as a tactical means of warning the enemy to keep outside it or be attacked. There was some discussion in signals about what to call the exclusion zone. Was it a maritime exclusion zone or a total exclusion zone? We needed a decision from the top to avoid any possible confusion. The relevant signal duly arrived, I believe, from the sharp-witted Vice-Admiral Sir David Hallifax, the Chief of Staff to the Commander-in-Chief of the Fleet. It consisted of just two words, 'Tis Tez'.

The arrival of the carriers meant we had about two days during which we could rehearse our air defence role, their Sea Harriers providing us with targets on which we could practise locking our missile-control radars and guns. *Coventry*'s fighter control officer, Sub-Lieutenant Andy Moll, also needed practice in controlling the missile-armed Harriers and directing them towards enemy aircraft. By this time, we were no longer hiding our presence and so could transmit on all our radars and communication nets, enabling us to carry out vital testing and tuning. Every weapon, radar and piece of equipment had to be operating satisfactorily, and all the skills and experience of the technicians and maintenance personnel were required to keep our systems in good working order.

Coventry's nerve centre, effectively her eyes and ears, was the operations room in the heart of the ship on 2 deck, where banks of consoles and screens gave the captain a picture of the current air, surface and underwater situation. It was from here that all the weapons were controlled, and every piece of information gleaned by the ship's sensors or from incoming signals and data links from other ships was displayed. The compartment was dimly lit and there was always an air of concentration as the team of over thirty people monitored their screens and equipment. It required very close teamwork and much practice to assimilate all the data and present it to me in good time so that I could make my decisions. I would be listening on the internal circuits to my two key warfare officers (the air warfare officer and the principal warfare officer) as the picture developed and any threat emerged. It was a process of continual discussion and assessment but sometimes it had to be quick and decisive. I had complete confidence in the entire team – which was just as well: we could certainly not afford to have any weak links here if the ship was to fight effectively and survive.

There were two air warfare officers – or anti-air warfare officers to give them their full title – who alternately kept watch in the operations room during weapons training exercises or in wartime. They were Lieutenant-Commanders Dick Lane and Mike O'Connell. The ship also carried two principal warfare officers who also took turns in watch-keeping: Lieutenants David Walton and Clive Gwilliam. Two specialist warfare officers, one of each, were always on watch together at busy times, one concentrating solely on the air threat and the other on the surface and sub-surface threat. Clive Gwilliam had served with me in *Hampshire* some seven years before and I felt fortunate to have him on board. Predictably, he proved to be very tough and capable, and he contributed a great deal to our warfighting efficiency. These warfare officers were the leaders of the two alternating crews in the operations room, and there was always a healthy rivalry between the two crews as to which was the most effective or had inflicted the most damage on the enemy.

On each side of the operations room was a door leading into a main passageway, also on 2 deck, which ran almost the full length of the outer perimeter of the ship, on both sides, from the bows to the quarterdeck. Off each passageway on the same level were doors into various compartments including living spaces (mess decks) and offices. There were also watertight hatches with ladders down from the passageways to other compartments such as store rooms, more mess decks and machinery spaces; these were mostly on 3 deck, though the larger machinery spaces went down to 4 deck level, well below the waterline. In a compartment directly below the operations room, linked to it by a hatch and a ladder, was the computer room on 3 deck: it was from here that all the information for the weapon controls and visual displays in the operations room was generated.

The two passageways, port and starboard, were themselves divided into sections by watertight doors spaced about every thirty feet along their length. They would enable any damage, fire or flooding to be contained and controlled. In a peacetime cruising situation, when the doors and hatches could be left open, the passageways were always busy as access could be gained from them to any compartment or part of the ship by many ladders, up or down. At action stations, most of the many watertight doors and hatches in the ship had to be tightly closed to enable the ship to sustain damage and keep fighting, and we needed to be very efficiently organized to achieve this in the shortest possible time.

The readiness of the ship and the crew for action was anyway soon to be tested, as by now the diplomatic negotiations had failed and war was imminent. The Admiral signalled us to be in all respects ready for war by midnight on 29 April and shortly afterwards he ordered *Coventry*, *Sheffield* and *Glasgow* – now formed about twenty miles ahead of the carrier group – to cross into the exclusion zone the next day. The three Type 42 destroyers were on picket duty, out in front of the carriers and closest to the direction from which enemy aircraft were likely to approach. We were there to detect and, of course, to deal with any threat before these highly valuable ships of the main force could be harmed. Our radars could see beyond 200 miles, and so if we saw aircraft heading towards us, we had the time to direct the Harriers to intercept them or to take them on with our own missiles.

The air battle could not be won without the two carriers and their Harrier fighters, of which there were twenty at this stage. The carriers also had helicopters embarked: most were for anti-submarine protection but others equipped with electronic listening equipment and radar were earmarked to assist in providing early warning of enemy aircraft or missiles. There was little doubt that if the enemy remained in control of the air over the Islands, a landing force with all its amphibious shipping would not survive and the war would be lost. Currently, the Argentinian Air Force was operating from both the Islands, mainly from East Falkland at Stanley, and from their mainland air bases some 400 miles to the west where most of their aircraft were concentrated.

It seemed clear to us that the Carrier Battle Group's first vital mission must be to take out the runway at Stanley as well as all the airfield facilities and defences, and to deny the enemy their use. Then it was a question of taking on the Argentinian Air Force as a whole, reducing its effectiveness and gaining air superiority over the Islands. This was a daunting task and one which was bound to be costly. The carriers themselves could not be risked and therefore had to remain, in the early days at least, some 100 miles to the east of the Islands out of the range of the aircraft based on the mainland, particularly the Super Étendards. Our Amphibious Task Group and Landing Force Group, making their way from the UK, would have to remain well clear of the action while they assembled and rehearsed the complex and risky business of an opposed amphibious landing.

The task of the picket ship is a lonely one: you are out on your own, intentionally placed in harm's way, and you have plenty of time to contemplate the fate of both your ship and your crew. You are likely to be sunk first in any attack on the main force, and you are always a tempting target to a submarine, since a single ship is especially vulnerable. Such was my lot, but it was what the Type 42 had been designed to do, and so I wasn't complaining. Besides, we would probably be the first to have a chance to engage the enemy and that, at least, was an exciting prospect.

Finally, we were ready for war. On the morning of the Battle of Trafalgar in 1805, Nelson had composed a final prayer to God for 'a great and glorious victory, and may no misconduct in anyone tarnish it, and may humanity after victory be the predominant feature in the British Fleet'. Our own Admiral, alluding to Nelson's prayer, sent a final signal to stiffen us for the fight and settle our nerves. Then, in the early hours of 1 May, the Carrier Battle Group entered the exclusion zone. The war was about to begin.

CHAPTER 4

ON THE BRINK

After three long weeks of worry and uncertainty, it was a great relief when it became clear that there was now no alternative but to fight. Our anger mounted against this harsh and unpredictable enemy and we became united in our purpose. The faint-hearted became strong, the ship's company stiffened to the challenge and we went into battle, confident and, outwardly at least, cheerful.

We were grateful that we had been well trained and were in a good ship with an effective missile system, and we were very glad to be in company with other good ships. As ever, I was strengthened by the fact that I knew well all the other commanding officers with whom I would be working: I felt I was very much part of a tough, capable team whose members understood and supported each other. No one was going to let anyone else down; indeed, there was a strong sense that we were, in our way, a band of brothers, much like Nelson's captains before us. They, too, had known precisely what they had to do and what their admiral expected of them.

For my part, I was thankful that I had had considerable experience at sea in destroyers and frigates operating in various parts of the world and in many different situations. I had been able to observe how commanding officers performed in difficult circumstances and, I hoped, had learnt from their strengths as well as their weaknesses. As the navigating officer of a frigate operating in Icelandic and Arctic waters, I had learnt a great deal about ship-handling in the roughest of weathers. I had been well tested in a frigate in the Dartmouth Training Squadron, which had involved frequent manoeuvring in close company with other ships and navigating close to treacherous shores. In both these and other ships, in my capacity as the operations room officer, I had also frequently worked under pressure during rigorous exercises and weapons training. As a result, my confidence was high and, in this respect at least, I did not find it difficult to go to war.

In peacetime, a considerable amount of time is devoted to the day-to-day running of a ship. There are invariably issues concerning welfare, discipline and the training of personnel. There are exercises and weapon trials to be carried out, and defect reports to be written. Safety checks and inspections have to be made, and routine paperwork has to be dealt with. In times of war, however, all this has to be put aside: you have to change your mindset and concentrate totally on fighting and surviving. I was surprised at how very quickly I discarded the inhibitions and habits of peacetime; so many rules and regulations, so much bureaucracy and administration suddenly became irrelevant, and this lifted a huge burden off me. In many respects, my life seemed so much easier now.

I well remember receiving a rather brisk letter from an admin-

istrator in the Ministry of Defence chasing a response from me
on the results of a trial we had been conducting on some new
chairs in the ratings' dining room. How absurd this letter
seemed, and its timing could not have been worse. I just threw
it straight in the bin – and really enjoyed doing so. I needed to
concentrate on essentials and get at the enemy by whatever
means. And I no longer feared that I was being swept helplessly
down a river: I was simply following its course wherever it
might take me, and I was in full control.

The signal traffic was huge and there was much to read and
assimilate. The dissemination of intelligence took up much of
this traffic, along with an ever-increasing amount of information
about our own expanding forces and plans. I enjoyed reading
about the operations of the SAS, the tricks that they were going
to get up to ashore and how they were going to survive behind
enemy lines: there were sections in the briefs on how to make
contaminated water drinkable, which wild animals were best to
eat and how to cook them. It was good for our morale to know
that both the SAS and the Royal Marine Special Boat Service
(SBS) were there already and doing their best to soften up the
enemy. I was even given the book *Who Dares Wins*, the story of
the SAS, by one of my sailors following a discussion we had had
on the subject during a quiet moment on the bridge.

I was also reading a book about the Gallipoli campaign in the
First World War. Written by a naval officer who had been a
midshipman in charge of a landing craft, it was an horrific
account – and also a depressing reminder of how difficult it was
to put troops ashore on a strongly defended beach. I could not
help relating it to any similar operations we might be involved
in: I thought it unlikely that our troops would meet the same,

fierce resistance experienced from the Turks at Gallipoli, but I did think they would be extremely vulnerable to air attack unless we could substantially diminish that threat first. The landings of 1982 had the potential to be just as disastrous as those of 1915.

The intelligence on the enemy was, of course, invaluable. Information on the condition of the troops on the ground, their morale and training gave a comprehensive picture of their fighting qualities. They numbered about 10,000, but most were badly paid conscripts who were not greatly motivated to defend these windswept and rather forbidding islands. Nor were they well led by their officers. It was also encouraging to learn that the three Argentinian services did not get on well together and that there was much rivalry between the three commanders of the Navy, Army and Air Force – Anaya, Menendez and Lami Dozo respectively. None of them got on particularly well with Galtieri, the head of the junta, either, and whoever came out best in the war would no doubt lay a claim to his job. The conduct of the enemy's war was clearly not going to be as co-ordinated or effective as it could or should be.

All the evidence suggested that the cream of the Argentinian military was to be found among the pilots of the Air Force and the Navy. They possessed a distinct flair which reflected their Latin temperament and were to prove themselves dashing, brave and extremely patriotic. In fact, there was very much a Battle of Britain atmosphere at their air bases and morale among the pilots was very high – to begin with, at least. The Navy itself did not appear so well prepared. The *Veintecinco de Mayo* was not fully worked up and its speed was apparently restricted by defects, making it difficult for the carrier to get its aircraft off the decks safely, especially in light winds. The Type 42 destroyer built in South America had, I believe, a distorted keel – an inherent fault in its initial construction and one which affected the accuracy of its missiles and guns. In the event, the Navy proved generally cautious and not many of its ships ventured out far from their bases. This wariness may only have been increased by reported sightings early on of a British nuclear submarine off the Argentinian coast. This could, of course, have been a deliberate piece of disinformation on our part: we did have three nuclear submarines whose job it was to detect, shadow and report the movements of any naval vessel or submarine leaving the mainland bases; yet it is equally possible that all were still on their way from the UK. Such is the sinister deterrent power of the submarine.

Unlike, I suspect, many members of the Argentinian armed forces, I had every confidence in our own commanders: Admiral Lewin, Chief of the Defence Staff, Admiral Leach, First Sea Lord, and Admiral Fieldhouse, Commander-in-Chief of the Fleet. As this was first and foremost a maritime operation, we had all the right people at the right time. But Admiral Fieldhouse, the Task Force Commander at Northwood, and his senior commanders could not easily advise and bring their experience to bear if communication with those in the front line was poor. In this respect, satellite communications were vital and the links between the task groups at sea and headquarters at Northwood proved excellent: they were instant and secure from enemy eavesdropping, which meant that the Admiral in his flagship *Hermes* could talk in real time with the Commander-in-Chief. Similarly, we had secure communications between our ships and the flagship, and indeed between all ships. This was all extremely reassuring.

We owed the success of these communications to the Americans, who allowed us the continuing use of their satellites. This was a facility which had been granted to us and used before the conflict, but it could so easily have been switched off and denied us if the US had found itself under diplomatic or other pressures. The Americans also continued to supply us with Sidewinder missiles for our Harriers and allowed us the use of their air base on Ascension. But there was little else they could do to help as their important – and sensitive – relations with their South American allies had to be carefully maintained. It was therefore all the more vital for Britain to retain support for her actions and try and ensure that Argentina remained, in most countries' eyes, the aggressor. There was also a fear that Russia might become involved in the conflict, siding with the Argentinians and sending nuclear submarines to assist in sinking the big ships in the Task Force. I am not sure whether I really believed this was likely, even in the prevailing Cold War climate, but it was certainly discussed.

The sense of being part of a team, particularly with the other Type 42s, was only enhanced by the many communication links between the ships doing the fighting. In the operations room, my warfare officers had direct links with their counterparts in other ships. After hostilities started, I would listen on my headset and hear the familiar voices of the warfare officers in the other two destroyers in the air defence screen and the voice of the overall air warfare commander in *Invincible*. I would also hear the voices of the pilots of the Harriers as we controlled them towards the oncoming enemy raids. The voices were almost conversational but at the same time urgent, clear, decisive and, on the whole, confident. It was a little like listening to a commentary on a very exciting football match, only the stakes were considerably higher.

I also had a direct link, if I wished to use it, with my fellow commanding officers, one that helped me clarify any uncertainties we might have about a particular threat or the position of a target. Later on, I would often be summoned to talk to the Admiral directly. He would brief me precisely on what he wanted me to do and then send me on my way, invariably following up the verbal instruction with a signal so that I had everything clearly in writing. I would detect in his voice a mixture of encouragement, sympathy and reluctance. Before *Coventry* undertook her final – and particularly dangerous – mission, he even attempted to reassure me by saying, 'Don't worry, we have knocked down all their experienced pilots; there's only the second eleven left.' I appreciated the gesture, as I think Sandy Woodward found it quite hard to send us off to confront a determined enemy at close quarters. Perhaps it was because he would rather have liked to have been doing the job himself: he had commanded *Sheffield* a few years before and so knew the ropes. It was not his natural inclination to be in the flagship, which was necessarily about a hundred miles to the east of the Falklands and more or less out of harm's way. Anyway, I was glad to have detected a soft spot in my boss, who seemed to many to have a rather cold and hard exterior. He was human after all.

A vital element of our communications was some special equipment that had recently been fitted in *Coventry*. It was designed to listen to enemy signal transmissions and had been fitted in my ship because, had events in the South Atlantic not intervened, in the summer of 1982 we would have been sent on an intelligence-gathering mission monitoring Soviet naval activities in the Barents Sea. I had overlooked the equipment until, out of the blue, a helicopter hovered over the quarterdeck and delivered up three senior ratings and a sergeant of the Royal Air Force, led by Chief Petty Officer Brian Mallinson, who were qualified Spanish interpreters. I met them as they staggered along the lurching deck and held on for dear life. It was difficult to get a smile out of them at this point, but they were later to do a wonderful job in infiltrating the enemy air waves and providing me with warning of air attacks as they built up: we seemed to know everything that was going on at the mainland air bases, and could even hear senior Argentinian commanders talking and arguing with each other.

As we entered the war zone, most men rose almost overnight to the challenges and dangers. Young sub-lieutenants found themselves conning the ship while we refuelled alongside darkened tankers on the blackest of nights and in the dirtiest of weather, and they performed the task magnificently. The first lieutenant often took command of the ship for a few hours in the night so that I could get some sleep. I was getting to know my officers and key senior ratings very well, and also their strengths and weaknesses. I began to notice how some people were not as good as others at coping with the stresses of war. In fact, I was surprised that some apparently robust individuals were not measuring up terribly well, while others, who had seemed less impressive, were coming into their own. Now, though, I badly needed strong and positive characters around me, and in this respect I was not to be disappointed.

It was unknown territory for us all, and until the first disaster occurred, we could not begin to imagine what the horror of war was really like. Besides, there was always the hope that it would never happen to you. Such expectations, however tenuous in reality, are actually very strong in war, and they may well stop you dwelling too much on the calamities which might befall you. Yet they encourage a rather perilous state of mind – one which, I suspect, prevails among all but the really battle-hardened. On the one hand you keep going, however dangerous the fighting might be. On the other, you may be tempted to take just one risk too many. It is all very much a double-edged sword.

One essential to grasp from the start was that you were on your own. It was little use worrying the flagship with your problems or expecting that a badly needed spare part was just going to appear, as if by magic. You could ask for stores and spares, but in the heat of war you might not receive them. You had to fix things yourself, and so ingenuity and initiative were the order of the day. On one occasion, we somehow repaired our defective long-range radar in the middle of an air raid by using the elements of a toaster from a mess deck. Miracles were achieved by the engineers as they overcame serious defects which would normally have merited a return to harbour. Even the ship's doctor had to be a dentist as well.

Once, in lieu of a vital spare part I needed to rectify a fault in our towed decoy noise-maker, I received via the special delivery helicopter a large and brand-new fridge. There must have been a mix-up in the code numbers and I never did receive the spare. The fridge, however, went straight over the side: there was simply no room for it on board. But the purpose of the noise-maker was to deflect torpedoes, and I knew that the enemy's 209-class submarines carried torpedoes with extremely powerful warheads designed to explode a few feet under a ship's keel. The resulting upward force of the water could break a destroyer like *Coventry* in half, and it would then go down in minutes. From then on, therefore, whenever I had a bath at night, I did so in very quick time: I really did not want to be caught in it if the ship was hit – something I knew had happened to more than one commanding officer in the Second World War.

On another occasion, later on, I sent the flight commander in our helicopter to the flagship to collect a spare part and in the process he observed some of the Navy and RAF pilots who had just arrived with their ground-attack Harriers transported down in the *Atlantic Conveyor*. It was not an encouraging sight. These pilots were young and straight out of initial training; they had never flown from carriers before or even over the sea. Yet they were to be shown around the ship, their first, briefed about the enemy and sent into battle the next day. They flew with a more experienced pilot, to begin with anyway, and undertook one practice night-flying sortie, but that was all. In fact, even some of those more experienced pilots had not flown the Harrier before: they had been pulled out of exchange posts in the USA and Australia and flown back to the UK to train on an aircraft whose single greatest asset – its VSTOL capability – meant that it had to be handled very differently to conventional jets, especially at take-off and on landing. The Harrier pilots seemed altogether a rather motley crew. But I need not have worried: both they and their aircraft were to perform superbly and make an absolutely crucial contribution to our victory.

Assembling the vital ingredients of this war – the personnel and all manner of hardware and resources – was difficult enough. But then everything had to be conveyed thousands of miles down to the wild South Atlantic, in preparation for an arduous campaign. It seemed an almost impossible task. None the less, we were always greatly encouraged when we learnt of even more ships being prepared to join us and then steaming down to support us in a wide variety of roles. About fifty 'ships taken up from trade' or STUFT vessels were requisitioned for the campaign, yet these additions to our fleet, however welcome, also emphasized the seriousness of the situation. Heavy repair and hospital ships were among the long train of vessels now ploughing through the South Atlantic, and it was clear what they were coming to do.

The SS *Atlantic Conveyor*, commanded by Merchant Navy Captain Ian North, was a STUFT ship owned by Cunard and converted at Devonport dockyard to operate helicopters. She was an 18,000-ton container carrier with a roll-on-roll-off capability and transported Harriers, Chinook and Wessex helicopters, as well as many aircraft spare parts. Her cargo could not have been more vital to the war effort, as was that of the other ships taken from trade for this operation. Similarly, the war could not have been won without the ever-present Royal Fleet Auxiliary Service ships. This is a civilian-manned fleet owned and operated by the Ministry of Defence. Its task is to supply warships of the Royal Navy at sea with fuel, food, stores and ammunition so that they can remain operational away from shore bases. The RFA also provides aviation and amphibious support.

Among the RFAs who kept *Coventry* supplied with all its needs was RFA *Fort Austin*, a vessel I was to see much more of as the weeks went by. She was a fast fleet replenishment ship, able to carry and transfer at sea all types of naval and victualling stores and ammunition. With her troops and helicopters

embarked at Ascension, she played a vital role in the recapture
of South Georgia and was later in San Carlos Water, where
she endured the nightmare of the bombings while supporting the
Amphibious Task Group. Wherever the naval ships went,
the RFAs went too and many were in the thick of the action. Sadly,
they were also to experience their share of tragedy, when the
RFAs *Sir Galahad* and *Sir Tristram*, both logistic landing ships,
were attacked at Bluff Cove.

The impressive list of ships heading south, written up on the
signal board on the bridge of *Coventry*, seemed to embrace
nearly the whole of the Royal Navy: it surely represented a huge
enterprise, one which was clearly going to stretch the Navy to
its limits. I noticed that Petty Officer David Nuttall, the Yeoman
of Signals, had mischievously added the names *Victory* and
Mary Rose to the list to amuse us: they were, in fact, probably
the only two ships left in Portsmouth. (*Mary Rose*, once the
flagship of the Tudor fleet, was then in the process of being
recovered from the seabed after lying there for over four
centuries.)

The yeoman, along with his team of radio operators, was
responsible for all the tactical signalling, which kept him on
the bridge for long periods when the ship was manoeuvring
in company with other ships. His operators, transmitting and
receiving signals between ships, would relay the messages and
instructions through him to the captain and officer-of-the-watch.
He would always know the disposition of ships around us and
the position that *Coventry* was to maintain. One of his team,
Radio Operator Tim 'Trev' Trevarthen, was a bright and lively
nineteen-year-old who had many friends on board. It was
difficult for anyone to be dispirited for long in his company,

especially if you found yourself on the bridge during his many hours of watch-keeping there. He was typical of the young men in the ship, many of whom were the same age or even younger.

Yeoman Nuttall's colleague, Petty Officer Sam MacFarlane, the radio supervisor, managed the more technically trained radio operators and equipment in the main communications office on 2 deck. This was close to the operations room and was where he processed a vast quantity of the more strategic signal traffic, including intelligence reports. I would have a thick file of new signals to read every morning and evening to keep myself up to date with what was going on. Communications were the key to everything and these two senior ratings bore the great responsibility between them, answering directly to the communications officer, Lieutenant Ray Adams.

Helicopters performed a multitude of tasks aside from their primary war roles. They flew over considerable distances in all weathers, and even while the enemy was active in the air, delivering mail, personnel and stores to ships. I often watched them hovering over the quarterdeck as *Coventry* heaved about in a rough sea, balancing on the very air itself, or so it seemed, and rising up and down in time with the ship. This demanded considerable skill, especially in the turbulent winds which rattled down the ship's side and over the quarterdeck, whipping up great volumes of spray in the process.

At one stage *Antrim*'s veteran Wessex helicopter had reason to make a delivery to *Coventry*. This transpired to be none other than the affectionately named 'Humphrey', the helicopter that I had known when I was in *Hampshire* and had taken me on that emotional visit in 1976 to Nevis to visit my father's grave. I realized that it was my old friend because it was the custom that wherever Humphrey went a red sticker in the form of both a hippopotamus and, with only a little exaggeration, the helicopter itself would be attached to some conspicuous object as a kind of calling card. One of these stickers, so familiar from the past, was presented to me after the transfer and it gave me something to smile about: I think someone must have known that I was an old admirer of Humphrey's. In fact, I was even more of an admirer now because this particular helicopter had just played a key part in the recapture of South Georgia and, in the process, had crippled the Argentinian submarine *Santa Fé* with depth charges. In my next letter home to the girls, I placed the sticker at the top of the sheet of writing paper, hoping to amuse them a little. 'Humphrey' survived the war and is now permanently on display in the Fleet Air Arm Museum at Yeovilton.

The arrival of mail by helicopter was a highlight of the day and it was quickly distributed. The sailor on board who combined his duties with those of postman always ensured that the ship's company's letters were ready at short notice for the next helicopter. He also went to the trouble of both designing and producing a rubber stamp which showed a penguin carrying a white ensign over its shoulder with the words 'HMS *Coventry* Falklands 1982' around it. This image was duly stamped in red ink on the back of all outgoing envelopes. It was a lovely idea, not least because it reminded everyone that even a situation like ours could have a lighter side.

I used to write quick letters home whenever I could to ensure that they would be available for collection when that next helicopter duly arrived. I remember doing some drawings with my letters for Miranda and Alice, usually showing the ship in action letting off salvoes of missiles and guns at aircraft. I am not sure what they made of them: they might even have thought I was having a lot of fun. In return, I received drawings showing me standing on the deck of my ship with captions such as 'Hi, captain!' and 'Mind you don't fall overboard!'. Miranda even did a drawing of *Coventry* to give to my Petty Officer Steward, Mick Stuart. He was very touched and pinned it up on the wall in the pantry.

My letters from home, apart from family news, told me what was going on in the wider world and reminded me how strongly the nation was rallying to the cause. What a difference this was going to make, for wars are not easily won by nations if they are divided or unconvinced as to the rightness of their cause. D herself had taken on the role of getting together the wives of my officers and men in the Portsmouth area to help comfort and inform them as much as she could. She became a reassuring and helpful contact for many, although, given her own anxieties about me, this could not have been easy for her. But she, in turn, had other friends in similar circumstances who supported her.

Like others, I suspect, I wrote a last letter home in case I did not survive and I sent it to Richard Luce for him to give to D in that eventuality. This was probably a rather tactless thing to have done as my brother-in-law had just resigned from the government and he might have felt some responsibility for my being sent to the Falklands to assist in resolving the problem by force. I very much hope he did not, for he had no reason to.

This letter was written on 24 April and it began: 'If you get this letter, I have slipped quietly beneath the waves and am utterly at peace in the next world. Please try very hard not to be too sad, although I know it will be difficult. Remember, I will always be aware when you are sad and I will always be trying very hard to make sure you remain happy for the rest of your life. I will always be with you . . . Look to the future and your life with the girls – this may mean marrying again if it's the way to a happy and fulfilled life for you all. For this reason, it will have my full blessing . . . Be brave, talk about me and laugh about me and always remember I am still around . . .'

I did not find it a particularly difficult letter to write: it entirely fitted the mood of the moment and was something one just wanted to do. After all, life was fast becoming somewhat tenuous. I had, inevitably, to romanticize my death, since in reality I was far more likely to be burnt to a cinder or blown to bits. Although it cannot always be much fun for those receiving them, I think people generally write rather good letters in these predicaments and also that they feel better for having written them. I certainly did. As it was, D was given my letter by her brother some time later, by which time I was safely back at home. In due course, she told me that she had read it, but only cursorily: other things had seemed to matter rather more at the time.

No formal suggestion was made to the officers and men that they should consider writing a last letter home in the event of their not surviving and, apart from the first lieutenant, I am not aware of anyone who did. All were advised to write their wills, though, if they hadn't already and to post them home, and this might perhaps have prompted some to include a letter of farewell. Obviously, this was a deeply private matter and anyway no one would have wanted to admit that their own death was even a possibility. I didn't feel any great sense of foreboding or gloom about my chances of survival – indeed, at this stage I don't think I really believed we were in too much danger. None the less, we were still embarking on a shooting war with all the attendant risks, and I suppose I was keen to put my affairs in order.

Initially, I had found it hard to come to terms with the fact that we were going to war. Others, I think, must have found it a great deal harder. Seaman Mick Daniels, a sonar operator, had been in the ship for over two years. He had now decided to leave the Navy and so our visit to Gibraltar and the ensuing exercise would be his swansong: he would then return to Portsmouth a day before his birthday on 7 April and enter civvy street. But now he learnt that he was on his way to fight in a war in the South Atlantic. Daniels was dismayed, to say the least. He asked his divisional officer, Sub-Lieutenant David Cooke, what his chances were of getting back to the UK. Non-existent, came the reply, whereupon he realized that the Navy was going to get its last ounce of flesh out of him.

'My attitude changed,' Daniels wrote later in his reminiscences, 'when the reality of the situation dawned on me, and then I wanted to complete the job for which I had trained so hard. I started to keep a daily diary which I kept in my respirator bag and carried around. Who could forget filling out their will forms? Or helping to paint the big black stripe down the ship's side? What a target for attacking planes . . . Now I carried my emergency tin opener and a small can of rice pudding around with me everywhere, along with plasters, a bandage and little pack containing my wallet, prisoner-of-war card, and some emergency money – all contained within a waterproof plastic bag. They were all essential items, as would be proved later.'

Coventry's sonar team was small – some twelve men – and efficient, and in Petty Officer Michael 'Foxy' Fowler, it had a father figure who took excellent care of those in his charge. Mick Daniels was going to survive. Michael Fowler, however, was not.

CHAPTER 5

AT WAR

The war began on 1 May. The British Carrier Battle Group was now well inside the exclusion zone, and the three Type 42s were out in front on their picket stations, *Coventry* to the south-west, *Glasgow* in the middle and *Sheffield* to the north-west. We knew that our Harriers had to succeed against the Argentinian Air Force if we were to gain the upper hand and knock the enemy's confidence straightaway: if we suffered losses, they would be back the next day with their tails up and the scales might tip against us.

It was our job to direct the Harriers towards the enemy aircraft which were operating over East Falkland in defence of the airfield and their own troops. We could actually hear the desperate dogfights taking place and, unsurprisingly, we could also detect the fear in the voices of our pilots, who were very tense and nervous on this first day of the conflict. But they did brilliantly: I believe two Mirages, three Skyhawks and three Canberras were shot down. Already the Harriers had proved their worth, and none was lost. It could not have been a better start.

A number of Harriers went in to bomb the runway at Stanley and the aircraft on the ground there, while others stood by to defend them and take on the enemy in the air. Almost every available Harrier took to the air to make the maximum impact. In advance of these Harrier attacks, a Vulcan bomber had dropped twenty-one 1,000-pound bombs on the airfield at about four o'clock in the morning local time. The massive and totally unexpected explosions must have been terrifying, and the realization that we could bomb the Islands with such a powerful aircraft operating from Ascension Island must have given the Argentinian commanders much to think about.

In fact, the damage inflicted by the Vulcan was limited to one large hole halfway down and on the centre line of the runway, but this put paid permanently to the chances of the Argentinians' fast fighter aircraft landing there to refuel and rearm. This, in turn, meant that these aircraft could now only fly from the mainland to attack the main Carrier Battle Group and had to return there directly; the amount of time they could spend in the vicinity of the Islands engaging British aircraft and ships was therefore much reduced. Air-to-air refuelling might have solved this problem, but the Argentinians had not developed or practised this sufficiently, at least not in the early stages of the war.

The operation to get a Vulcan to the Falkland Islands was a truly amazing feat, involving a round trip from Ascension of nearly 8,000 miles and six in-flight refuellings from Victor tanker aircraft. The limited number of hits achieved by the Vulcan with its rather antiquated bomb-aiming system was the best that could be hoped for, yet the damage to the enemy's morale and the effect on his future operations were out of all proportion to the physical damage inflicted. A second Vulcan raid took place a few days later, although on this occasion little damage was done and the airfield escaped any direct hits. Enemy aircraft did continue to fly from the airfield and from other small airfields on the Islands, but not the fighter jets, which was, of course, a huge benefit to us.

Further operations designed to make a dramatic and, we hoped, discouraging impression on the enemy included the bombardment with naval guns of the military infrastructure and concentration of troops around Stanley airport. The first ships to go in quite close to the shore south of the airport were *Glamorgan* and the frigates *Arrow* and *Alacrity*. These three ships used their 4.5-inch guns overnight and remained on station during the day to exploit any further opportunities to inflict damage on the enemy. All were attacked in daylight by Dagger aircraft which caught them by surprise as they came at them from off the land and at close range. The ships had little time to react and were hit by cannon fire but fortunately only suffered minor damage, although one sailor was quite seriously injured. It was a taste of things to come. Shortly after this, it was our turn to go in at night to bombard the airport area, which we did in company with *Broadsword*, a Type 22 frigate and sister ship of *Brilliant*. This was the first time we had gone in close to the shore and the enemy, and we were always relieved when we came away unharmed.

It was while working close to the coast that we caught our first glimpses of the Islands, usually through binoculars. Lieutenant Chris Pollard, who was to prove a great asset as the gunner responsible for the 20-mm guns and the small arms in the ship, scribbled a diary on the back of signals whenever he had a quiet moment and wrote rather unkindly about what he saw: 'As the sun rose at 1100 Greenwich Mean Time, we got our first glimpse of the Islands; what a dump it looks, like Wales on a wet Sunday after England have beaten them at Cardiff Arms Park and all the pubs have run out of beer, and it all smells of sheep droppings.' This forthright comment was entirely in character, although I suspect the lieutenant was tired and cold after a long watch and in no mood to appreciate anything he saw. In contrast, most of us thought the Islands looked rather beautiful, although in winter weather they appeared bleak and windswept. I regret that I never got ashore to have a look around and meet the Islanders who are nothing like their weather, being by all accounts very warm and friendly.

Broadsword came with us towards Stanley to provide some degree of protection with her modern short-range missile system Sea Wolf, which was designed to destroy attacking aircraft. Captain Bill Canning was her commanding officer and this was the first time I had worked with him. I had only met him once, and briefly, about a year earlier at one of our training establishments, but I soon came to value his experience and calm, reassuring presence. We were to work together even more closely after the landings by the amphibious force, but on this occasion we were positioned about seven miles to the south and west of the runway at Stanley. Unfortunately, we were only able to fire a very few shells as the turret of the 4.5-inch gun developed a defect. This was agonizingly frustrating and I felt I had failed miserably to do what was expected of me. We left at first light before any air threat materialized and raced back to the screen ahead of the carriers.

We returned to carry out more bombardment a day later and achieved better results. Our targets were the various military installations around the airfield. The SAS had by now carried out some useful reconnaissance behind enemy lines, providing us with detailed information about targets. This constant shelling of the airfield and installations such as artillery, radars and ammunition dumps would wear down the morale and fighting effectiveness of the enemy. In addition, the SAS were up to their usual tricks – setting off a random explosion here, leaving a discarded British cigarette packet there, and perhaps even adding something nasty to the water supplies. However, it was a risky business sending in ships so close to the shore, not only because of the shore batteries but also because of the skilfully piloted aircraft which flew so low over the hills and sprung out at you at such short range.

Some members of the SAS and SBS took passage in *Coventry* before being landed for their various missions. On one occasion, as they took some refreshments, they left an impressive array of small arms piled in the corner of the wardroom. I am sure the young Argentinian troops greatly feared the thought of going to sleep and waking up to feel the cold steel of a kukri or some other deadly blade at their throats. Word went around that some special forces personnel went so far as to 'liberate' the odd carving knife from the ship's galley before leaving, either to discard near their vacated campfires as an overt sign of their presence or to use more directly. For some members of the wardroom at least, this was a fascinating introduction to the rather different form of warfare then being waged ashore.

If we were not being sent off on other missions, *Coventry* was usually stationed in the south-west sector of the three-ship advanced screen some twenty miles ahead of the Carrier Battle Group, with *Sheffield* and *Glasgow* to the north of us. We were all becoming familiar with each other's voices on the communications networks and really getting into our stride as the first line of defence against the air threat. If we could continue to conduct the air battle at long range with the Harriers, then the enemy would be contained near East Falkland and away from the ships. It was, however, going to be touch and go, given the enemy's current superiority in the air, and we knew we were in for the long haul.

When dusk fell, the air threat would subside and this was to become the pattern for the weeks ahead. The Argentinians were not accustomed to flying over the sea and so they preferred to launch their attacks in daylight. When the sea was rough or visibility was low, they sometimes did not appear at all. All the same, we had to remain fully alert and were constantly testing our equipment and weapons. Technology in ships, particularly that associated with their automated systems, was not as reliable as it is now. Two of the most skilled of *Coventry*'s senior ratings, Chief Petty Officers Mick Burkmar and Keith Blenkharn, spent all their time, day and night, with the two 909 radars forward and aft to keep our Sea Dart guidance system correctly tuned. In this respect, the Type 42s were demanding ships, requiring a very high degree of skill to keep all their systems functioning – something you might not always be able to guarantee, especially on prolonged operations. There always seemed to be times when one ship or other had a defective radar or weapon, and this inevitably put a considerable strain on the others. Then there was the need every so often to make a dash back to the Battle Group to take on fuel or stores from the Royal Fleet Auxiliaries, and it was vital we spent as little time as possible out of the front line.

For a warship such as a destroyer or frigate to be effective, it needs to be both fast and capable of carrying a variety of weapons, radar arrays and aerials. Its hull should therefore be long and thin, as this configuration will give it a good turn of speed and provide sufficient space for weapons on the upper deck, magazines below decks and machinery spaces. A ship's length also determines its sea-keeping qualities and how well it can maintain speed heading into a rough sea as its bows slice through the waves: ideally, the hull should span several troughs of those waves. *Coventry* was one of the earlier Type 42s which, for reasons of economy, were built slightly shorter than they should have been. She could not therefore go fast into a heavy sea without pounding and getting the bows and the forward armaments very wet. The later Type 42s were a little longer and so performed better at speed. Consequently, as *Coventry* dashed about in bad weather, her forecastle (often referred to as fo'c'sle) was often awash with sea and the gun and the missile launcher would take a bit of a battering.

Sonar operator Able Seaman Paul Inman later wrote in his '*Coventry* Notes' of life on board at this time: 'Life during the war became a routine of on watch, off watch, action stations and replenishment at sea (RAS). We would eat when we could and sleep when we could. During one off-watch period, I decided I needed to have a shower as there was little opportunity to enjoy such luxuries – and, to the surprise of my mess-mates, I was going to have it whatever the consequences: no Argentinian was going to stop me. Fortunately, it all went without incident, I returned to the mess and climbed into my bunk – but at that very moment the action-station alarm sounded and I had to hurry back on watch.'

The ship's company were in two (defence) watches all the time, which meant that each person spent six hours on watch followed by six hours off. People generally became accustomed to this routine and, in theory at least, they could have survived several weeks of it. But when the ship went to action stations, everyone had to be on watch to man all the weapons effectively and deal with any damage, fire or first aid. Thus those who might have been getting their six hours of rest were often rudely interrupted. In addition, the general strain of war on top of the anxious and demanding month we had already spent at sea meant that a great deal of stamina, both mental and physical, was now required of everyone. None the less, we would try our best to replenish our fuel supplies from a tanker, for example, using just one watch of personnel so as not to disturb the other.

Missileman Able Seaman Richard Hopgood, who eventually rose to the senior position of master-at-arms in the Navy, wrote of these early days in the conflict: 'My defence watch was on the bridge as bosun's mate and I was able to get a good idea of what was going on, listening to the news on the bridge radio and ear-wigging on the officers' conversations. It was also interesting listening to the radio reports of the dogfights between the Harriers and the Argentinian aircraft. Whenever the captain came on to the bridge, it went quiet, not only because of the respect for him, but just in case he came out with some new piece of news. Some leaders rule by fear, by shouting, but that was not his style. He had the first lieutenant to do the barking, and bark he did.'

I was never one for shouting. In my experience, the commander who tends to shout at his officers and men is rarely a good leader: quiet professionalism sets a better example and achieves a more willing and effective response. I therefore always tried to maintain a calm presence on the bridge, and I disliked noise and rush about me. Indeed, whenever people did shout or rush, I would only become calmer: that way you made better decisions and you almost certainly made them faster. This is partly my nature: if someone were to throw a thunderflash which exploded at my feet, I doubt I would move very much. It is also common sense: sailors never run in ships, even when speedy action is called for, as panic and accident can easily follow.

Coventry's first lieutenant was Lieutenant-Commander Glen Robinson-Moltke, a gunnery specialist. He was responsible for the discipline of the ship's company as well as for running the day-to-day routine of the ship. He was himself a disciplined and organized individual who demanded very high standards. His job was a roving one – to get to know everyone, to encourage and lead, and to reprimand if necessary. It was right that he, rather than his captain, had the bark when it was needed, and in this respect he was just the right man to be my second-in-command. He astutely exercised a style of leadership which was very different to mine, and this proved the winning formula for a happy and well-run ship: in all my time on board, I cannot remember any disciplinary problems. Moreover, the organization that ensured the ship was manned and fought effectively was entirely his and could not have been achieved without either his considerable abilities or his dedication to the ship. He was very happily married to Christine from Denmark whose family name of Moltke was attached to his. They lived close to us in Petersfield and so we saw them from time to time socially, and Christine was to be a great help to D in helping to look after *Coventry* families.

As well as the air threat, we had to contend with the possibility of attacks from submarines and surface ships. The Battle Group deployed its anti-submarine Sea King helicopters on a screen well ahead of it with the aim of detecting and destroying any threat before an attack could be made on its most important ships, *Hermes* and *Invincible*. We often saw these helicopters moving between the positions at which they lowered their sonars into the water to listen for any movement of submarines. There was a screen, too, made up of several anti-submarine frigates which provided defence in depth and a shield for the Battle Group.

In our patrol area closest to the Islands, we took a particularly keen interest in the surface picture and plotted contacts reported by our aircraft or submarines on a large area chart in the operations room. In fact, right from the outset, we had kept the position of the heavily armed Argentinian cruiser, *Belgrano*, firmly on our plot, and as *Coventry* was the nearest ship to it, we had watched it closely. We had not thought the cruiser a threat as it was still outside the exclusion zone and, as far as we could tell, only making fairly slow progress in no particular direction. However, we had been warned of the possibility of a pincer movement developing whereby the carrier *Veintecinco de Mayo* and accompanying destroyers would approach the exclusion zone from the north-west and the *Belgrano* from the south-west, thus splitting our forces. One of our submarines was supposed to be keeping tabs on the carrier but, given the lack of reports, we had presumed it was having difficulty gaining contact in the shallow waters near the mainland.

Then, on 2 May, we had heard that the *Belgrano* had been sunk to the south-west of the Falkland Islands. This came as a real shock, and initially I feared that our action had been politically damaging: the ship had not been inside the exclusion zone and so by sinking it we had risked losing much of the international support which London had been working so hard to win on the diplomatic front. We badly needed allies in the prosecution of the war who would supply us with any additional arms, facilities or intelligence we might need – or who at the very least would not render the Argentinians any such assistance. But it was not for me to be dwelling on such matters: the deed had been done and, besides, I now had the satisfaction of clearing this potential troublemaker off my plot.

I was to learn more about the decision to sink the *Belgrano* later. I understand that Commander Chris Wreford-Brown, the captain of the submarine *Conqueror* who was trailing the cruiser and had it in his sights, was concerned that he might lose contact when it passed over the Burdwood Bank. The *Belgrano* was clearly heading towards these shallower waters, and this would make it both difficult for the submarine to manoeuvre and nearly impossible for its sonar to maintain contact amidst the turbulence and reverberations that occur in such waters. Wreford-Brown reported this to the Admiral in *Hermes* and the Task Force Commander, requesting further instructions.

But in war you must seize every opportunity. *Belgrano* posed a serious threat with its heavy guns and powerful missiles, and it says a great deal about the effectiveness of both satellite communications and our command structure that the *Conqueror* received the order to sink the ship with the authority of both the Prime Minister and the Task Force Commander in a very short space of time. We now know, of course, that the *Belgrano* was indeed part of a coordinated plan to engage the Carrier Battle Group from two different directions. The *Veintecinco de Mayo* to the north-west had sailed to launch an attack, but the winds were too light for the Skyhawks to be catapulted off the decks with a full bomb load and sufficient fuel to reach their targets and return safely. The carrier and its escorts then abandoned their mission and returned to coastal waters, where they remained for the duration of the war. At the same time as the planned carrier attack, the Super Étendards based at Rio Grande were to carry out an Exocet attack on the Battle Group from the south-west. The *Belgrano* was in a holding position during these two air operations, although she intended to steam in towards the Battle Group and attack with guns and her own Exocets in the immediate aftermath of the onslaught from the air. But the Super Étendards, dependent on in-flight refuelling to get them to the Battle Group, had to return to base when for some reason the refuelling failed. Thus an attack which might have had dire consequences failed to materialize.

As Able Seaman Richard Hopgood was to write later: 'The reality and danger of war hit home the evening the *Belgrano* was sunk. We all had quiet moments to ourselves, and I remember thinking about how I would fare in a situation like that – the fear, the dark, the cold and the sea. I felt some sorrow for the sailors on *Belgrano*, even though they were supposedly the enemy. But there was also some relief and joy that one of the enemy's major ships had been sunk.'

These were strange days. The war had begun and seemed to be going our way, but we were still naïve in many respects and far from battle-hardy. We had not yet suffered any losses ourselves. When we did, things would change.

CHAPTER 6

CHANGING
FORTUNES

In the first few days of the war, the Argentinians confined their air attacks to the area around the Islands and these were dealt with by the Harriers at some distance from us. Our greatest fear, however, remained the Exocet, the French anti-ship missile that was carried by the enemy's Super Étendard strike aircraft. The Exocet, with its substantial, 364-pound explosive warhead, is a particularly lethal weapon. A cruising speed of 700 mph enables it to cover some twenty-five miles in two minutes, and its modus operandi reduces any telltale radar transmissions to an absolute minimum. The aircraft carrying an Exocet only has to switch on its search radar for a moment or two in order to acquire a target and calculate its range and bearing – details which are fed into the missile's guidance system before it is launched. The Exocet then speeds on its way with no need to broadcast its presence: it is only when it closes the target that it activates its own radar, which locks on and holds the missile at sea-skimming height right up until final impact. All this conspires to make the Exocet very difficult to detect or deal with.

We had good intelligence on the missile: we knew that the Argentinian Navy had only five Exocets, and we even knew their serial numbers. Yet each could sink a ship, and so we would be keeping a very careful record of how many had been fired at us. There were, though, some counter measures available to us. We could, for example, turn the ship to a certain angle off the missile's approach course and then fire chaff from our rocket launchers which, with its millions of tiny metal needles, would create false radar echoes away from the ship. The ship had to be manoeuvred to stay within the pattern of the chaff, and this meant steaming at slow speed downwind. The missile would then be attracted to the false echoes rather than to the ship's echo reflected from the hull. This, at least, was both the theory and the hope. It all depended, of course, on our having detected the missile in the first place.

The anxieties of the warfare officers in the Type 42s can be easily imagined as they scanned their radars for likely Super Étendard contacts and listened to the electronic sensors tuned to detect the transmitting radar frequencies of the aircraft or of the missile itself. Sea King helicopters from the Carrier Battle Group were also equipped to detect the missile and they were positioned well forward in the likely direction of the threat: with their advantage of height, they hoped to gain the first detections and give early warning to the more vulnerable of our ships.

Both the weather and atmospheric conditions often played tricks with our radars and any number of spurious contacts would appear on our screens: it required a lot of skill and a level head to determine which of them was an enemy aircraft and which was not. Discussion on the air warfare circuits was often frantic as the operations room teams in the Type 42s compared notes and tried to sort out the true picture. Only then could missiles be directed to the right targets, and this could only be done provided we knew the positions of all our friendly aircraft. Although we received automatic transmissions from our own aircraft which produced a distinctive symbol on our radar displays, you still had to be absolutely certain you were firing at the enemy and not one of your own. In the heat of the moment, this was easier said than done.

We did not expect any threat from surface ships but as darkness descended one evening, a patrolling Sea King spotted a small warship to the north of the Islands. Being the nearest ship to it, we were ordered to despatch our Lynx helicopter armed with Sea Skua missiles. Directed by the Sea King, the Lynx gained contact and fired both missiles, scoring a direct hit. The ship, which was later identified as the Argentinian patrol vessel *Comodoro Somellara*, blew up and was destroyed: the explosion and subsequent fire could be heard and seen for miles around. As the Sea King looked for survivors, it came under fire from another similar ship, the *Alférez Sobral*. A Lynx from *Glasgow* was called up and its Sea Skuas also hit their target, causing severe damage and many casualties.

This was the first action we had carried out with the new and untried Sea Skua missiles we had hastily embarked off Ascension Island. When the Lynx returned from its mission, I went down to the quarterdeck to congratulate the flight commander and the pilot, Lieutenant-Commander Alvin Rich and Lieutenant Hubert Ledingham. Both were shocked and shaking, no doubt with relief at their safe return but also with the realization of what they had just done. They were now getting used to being at war.

Coventry was involved in another surface action when, one nightfall, we formed up with *Glasgow* in very poor visibility to take on two small but fast-moving radar contacts which we thought were fast patrol boats. Both ships fired about twenty rounds of 4.5-inch shell each and we 'destroyed' the targets: at any rate, there was no longer anything to be seen on our radar screens. Later we realized that we must have been engaging a group of albatross, which were often to be seen in these waters. Yet this had felt like a very real action and in war any contact which is not a known friendly unit is attacked without hesitation. In this case, the unusual atmospheric conditions had conspired to create false but all too realistic targets.

The next day was 4 May. We had been having trouble with our long-range radar and so was moved from the south-west sector of the screen to the north-west, where the air threat was least likely. We then got on with repairs while *Sheffield* took our place. It was a hectic day and started badly when one of our ground-attack Harriers, on a mission to destroy airfield facilities and aircraft on the ground, was shot down by heavy artillery and its pilot killed. Our luck was beginning to desert us.

Worse was to follow. *Coventry* and *Glasgow* got wind of a possible Exocet attack by Super Étendards from the south-west via our passive sensors although we had no confirmed contacts on radar. *Glasgow* soon became convinced that an attack was developing and even countermanded the senior air warfare coordinator in *Invincible*, who was insisting there was no such threat. There had been much anxiety earlier in the day as everyone tried to differentiate between possible aircraft contacts and a host of false echoes created, once again, by the prevailing atmospheric conditions. The sky was overcast, visibility low and the sea reasonably calm. *Sheffield* seemed unsure about the situation but we three screening ships kept talking to each other to try and ascertain exactly what was happening. *Coventry* and *Glasgow* fired chaff to create false echoes around their ships, something we were always quick to do whenever there was an inkling of a threat.

Suddenly there was silence from *Sheffield*. This was most unusual – for a second or two, I even thought the ship must have suffered a communications failure – and we presumed that we were under some sort of attack. Then we heard that *Sheffield* had been hit by a missile. It had slammed into her starboard side close to the waterline, creating an inferno of fire and smoke and massive damage inside the ship. My thoughts immediately turned to Sam Salt, *Sheffield*'s captain, and I wondered whether he had survived. His father had been killed early in the Second World War while commanding a submarine in the Mediterranean and I earnestly hoped that his mother was not going to lose a son as well as a husband.

The pilot of the Super Étendard, from the Naval Air Command at Rio Grande, had come in very low, underneath *Sheffield*'s main radar beams. He had popped up to have a look on his radar, and the moment he had seen an echo, he had fired. He had made no attempt to identify the target before he did so and had flown straight back to base after releasing his Exocet: when he landed, he was not even sure that he had hit anything. In fact, there had been two Super Étendards on this mission, each carrying one missile, but the other aircraft's missile had failed and crashed into the sea.

Twenty members of *Sheffield*'s crew were killed, and when the fire got out of control, the ship had to be abandoned. The next day she was taken in tow as a burnt-out wreck and eventually sank. *Yarmouth* (Commander Tony Moreton) and *Arrow* (Commander Paul Bootherstone) went alongside as she was still burning to rescue the survivors. Some were taken to *Hermes* by helicopter but eventually all were taken to Ascension by sea and then flown back to England.

Sam Salt, who survived unharmed, could not possibly have been blamed for this tragedy. With the ships and weapons at our disposal, designed for a very different war, we were always going to be doing it the hard way. (That, unfortunately, has all too often been the way of the British in war.) Sam was an inspirational leader and highly regarded throughout the Navy. But an Exocet travelling at hundreds of miles an hour and skimming the sea's surface below the reach of *Sheffield*'s radar coverage – and doing so at precisely the same time as the ship's detection equipment, through a technical limitation, failed to pick up the fleeting radar transmissions from either the aircraft or the missile itself – was bound to get through. And it would only have needed a momentary lapse in concentration on the part of one of the warfare team in the operations room to miss a vital piece of information – that tiny, flickering radar echo – which would then have triggered the alarm. Such is the nature of warfare in the missile age.

Eighteen-year-old missileman Able Seaman Martin 'Izzy' Isaacs, who was on watch on *Coventry*'s bridge, later recalled: 'I was on the bridge and remember the report of an air raid building up, and then a radio operator from *Sheffield* coming over the air in plain language and screaming, "We've been hit!" We all felt the fear. Obviously we went straight to action stations and scanned the skyline for any sign of her. We saw the thick black smoke on the horizon but could see no sign of the ship herself. We were all stunned.'

Radio Supervisor Sam MacFarlane also recorded his impressions: 'I was completely shattered and not a little scared. My friend and I had served on *Sheffield* not too long ago and had many good friends still there; waiting to see the list of survivors was an unbelievably hard task. We suffered together checking off those friends' names, with a smile for those who had survived but tears for those listed as dead. A horrible realization that they could after all get at you too was hard to accept amidst the sadness of this terrible loss. Memories of the good times on the "Shiny *Sheff*" flooded to the fore.'

The effect of the loss of *Sheffield* on my ship's company was devastating. Hardly a word was spoken for several hours and people had to struggle to overcome their feelings and fears. At the end of the day, Petty Officer Steward Mick Stuart came into my cabin and with noticeable emotion remarked, 'It has been a bad day today, sir.' 'Yes,' I replied, 'it has been a bad day.' It was all we could bring ourselves to say and even those few words were difficult enough. It was hard to talk without giving away one's fears, and anyway, we were too preoccupied.

Although we had all been abruptly shocked into reality, we were becoming battle-hardened ourselves, and twenty-four hours after that first grievous loss, we were no longer gloomy, our confidence returned and we became even more determined to hit back at the enemy just as soon as we could. War, after all, is a nasty business and those involved in it rarely display much sympathy towards the enemy or remorse after inflicting horror and death upon him. I certainly had no such feelings or regrets whenever I knew I had been responsible for causing death among my opponents: like most people's, my own survival instinct was strong and ensured that I remained ruthlessly single-minded. When it was all over, there would be plenty of time for reflection and understanding, and to express sympathy for the losses incurred on both sides – and I think reconciliation with former enemies is essential for the stability and peace of the world. But for now, I am sad to say, it was all about killing people and destroying aircraft and ships with the utmost vigour.

There was an absolute belief in the ship's company that our cause was just and their loyalty to the ship and to me was as firm as a rock. I could sense this at every turn, which was very good for my own morale. All we wanted to do was to win the war and get home. In fact, thoughts of returning to Portsmouth to a heroes' welcome were highly motivating, and I became acutely aware that nearly 300 people were depending on me to get them back safely. When trying to find something encouraging to say in one of my regular broadcasts to the ship's company, I told them that my holiday was booked from 4 August – which it was – and so we would be sure to be home by then. Out of this statement arose an almost mystical belief that, no matter what happened, we would be back by then – because the captain had said so. This had been, I suppose, the first time a date had been mentioned for our return home and so it provided an aiming point in people's minds which, when considering all the dangers and the uncertainties we faced, must have given some reassurance. It was such a small gesture and August still was a long way off, but even a hint of good news in war can make all the difference.

I sent a telegram to D at this time: 'Am very well, do hope you are all pottering along as usual, no need for any concern, hopefully back before too long, very much love.' I wondered whether this was at all helpful. I was obviously trying to play things down and sound relaxed about the situation, but stating that there was no need for any concern clearly indicated that there was. Once again, I think I must have felt better for sending it, and I could only hope that D did when she received it.

We certainly could not help thinking of the acute anxiety that our families must have been feeling after the *Sheffield* disaster, but it was a fairly fleeting thought for me as I was simply so busy. It was, in a way, far less difficult for me being at war and doing my job than it was for my wife and children, who were helpless onlookers. I was glad that the letters D and others wrote from 7 May onwards never reached me while I was in *Coventry*, as they would have been extremely hard to read in the heat of battle and would no doubt have caused me to worry unduly when I should have been concentrating on other things. But they at least survived: the inevitable delays and difficulties in delivering them to our ships meant that I only got them when I was either in *Stromness* or *QE2* on my way back to England.

D's letter of 7 May, which I did not receive until the end of the month, gave a strong feeling of what life was like at home: 'What a terrible week – after the dreadful shock we all felt over the sinking of *Sheffield*, one now feels quite numb and unable to believe it's happened. Your lovely telegram arrived the next day and was so calm and reassuring. What horror you must have all felt over it all, and the tragic loss of lives. Poor Sam Salt – a shattering experience – but thank God he was saved. I think the whole country was stunned and people have felt very emotional about it.

'And I hear the weather is really hellish now – you must be

simply worn out, being constantly on the alert in bad weather. Though we can imagine, none of us can really know what you are going through. How you ever get a wink of sleep I can't imagine. I hate this sort of war with horrible missiles – so much worse than sea battles of the last war when very often ships were able to limp back to port.

'Meanwhile at home I am so busy I feel quite dazed. I went to a meeting held by the Commodore of HMS *Nelson* [the naval barracks at Portsmouth] with commanding officers' wives and welfare workers. I am writing a letter which will be duplicated and sent to all *Coventry* families, and have arranged a meeting over tea at HMS *Sultan* [the Navy's engineering training establishment] for anyone who wants to come next Sunday. Nearly all ships are trying to get everyone together – with the link chaplains to help us. The Navy is being wonderful about the families – help from all directions.'

The gathering of families at *Sultan* in Gosport duly took place on 16 May, attended by a great number of wives, mothers, fathers and even one or two grandparents. They came to meet and share their anxieties with others and to find support, and they came from as far as Yorkshire, Wales, Norfolk and Devon. It was a friendly and comforting occasion which put many people in touch with each other, giving them some sort of a lifeline and a closer link with both D and the Navy. Even those who were unable to attend felt they had been drawn into the *Coventry* family through the correspondence surrounding the event.

Unsurprisingly, letters from my daughters brought a very different view on life. Miranda wrote: 'I am doing something called cycling proficiency. It is learning how to cycle on the roads and you have a test. There is a writing test which I passed and a cycling test which is on 10 May. I haven't done it yet because it is 8 May. It is very sad that *Sheffield* sank. Mrs Salt, the captain's wife, is coming to lunch today. P.S. I have got some new shoes.' I am quite sure she felt just as anxious about her cycling test as I did about being hit by missiles.

Following the attack on *Sheffield*, the Battle Group retreated more to the east for a period so as not to risk getting too close to the Islands, as it had done earlier when launching Harriers. Furthermore, these aircraft would not be used again in the ground-attack role while the Argentinian shore-based artillery remained effective, which it had certainly proved to be. The effect of the new positioning of the carriers meant that the Harriers would in future be operating close to their maximum range with only a comparatively short time available for engaging the enemy. This was not good news for me as we longed, especially in later operations, to have the Harriers in support for much longer. All the same, we could clearly see the necessity for the change.

While *Sheffield* was burning and being abandoned, and our ships were rallying round rescuing survivors or attempting to transfer stores and weapons from the wreck, it was thought that a submarine attack was developing. Ships were soon spotting periscopes all over the place and hurling mortar bombs in their direction. In the end, the flagship's senior warfare commander took charge, ordered the ships to calm down and to stop wasting their mortar bombs on a non-existent threat. It was clear that the commander of the Task Force had some good intelligence on the enemy submarines and that he knew by 4 May there was not going to be any danger from them. However, I realize now that he could not have told us for fear of giving away this information to the enemy and, consequently, the sources of his intelligence. Indeed, it was known that the two German-built submarines had been carrying out trials but also that they were having some problems with their torpedoes. It is possible that they did try and carry out attacks on our ships on the first day or two of the war, but evidently they were unsuccessful. The Argentinian Navy's two older submarines did not, I think, feature at all. None the less, right up to my last day in the conflict, I remained concerned about the threat from the modern submarines. I wish I had known the real situation, if only because I could then have stayed longer in my bath at night.

As it was, I wrote a quick letter to D on 6 May to put in an RFA which was going back to Ascension: 'I am quite safe and very well. It's not quite my scene, all this fighting – especially when I believe it could have been avoided. But that's a long subject which I shall expound on at length when I get back. Try not to worry – but I know you must be, terribly. Lovely to get your letters – last one written on 19 April.'

The days following the loss of *Sheffield* brought bad weather and poor visibility, both of which generally reduced the enemy's activity in the air. *Coventry*, however, remained alert as always, ready to detect and warn against any air threat. The task was more difficult without the third member of the Type 42 club and we now had to operate to the south of East Falkland, this being the most likely threat area. On 6 May we were in contact with two Harriers on patrol when they detected a suspicious surface contact on their radars: both descended to investigate. Suddenly we lost contact and there was complete silence. Nothing more was heard: the aircraft had simply disappeared. We learnt a short time later that they had crashed, probably after a collision with each other in the poor visibility. A search was carried out but neither aircraft nor pilots were ever found. We were now down to seventeen Harriers, and it would be some time yet before reinforcements would arrive from the UK in the merchant ship *Atlantic Conveyor*.

In another letter which I would not receive until much later, my brother-in-law Richard Luce wrote to me on 8 May: 'Rose and I are staying the night with D and the children and I thought I would write you a line. We have seen plenty of them all – indeed they stayed with us last weekend. D is in good form and very self-composed. She is getting on with a full life – apart from the children, the gardening seems to be very occupying. Naturally the hitting of *Sheffield* caused worries for all but I think we have all overcome the sadness and shock. So don't worry at all about D. The children really are in cracking form and I have just been playing duets with Miranda and D.

'We are all thinking of you a great deal and I can only imagine what it is like. But there is the greatest of admiration and support for you all amongst the public. I don't think any of us under-estimate the difficult nature of the task which you have been asked to perform. But it is a really important one and goes wider than just our country. I am having a very strange sabbatical which is self-enforced following my resignation and am taking full advantage of it. But of course I follow with great personal inter-est and anxiety everything that is happening over the Falklands. I will tell you the full story of the last few months when you return, and I shall look forward to hearing yours.

'I do hope you are getting enough sleep and are not too over-tired – I can imagine it is a continual strain on you all but I am sure you are all doing magnificently. In the meantime, you need not worry about D and the family. She is being marvellous and I shall continue to ring her regularly and to see her when I can. Good luck.'

As it happened, I was certainly not getting enough sleep by peacetime standards. Yet when the need dictates, you find you can get by quite happily with a good deal less. Excitement, anxiety and the responsibilities of rank all combine to ensure that you keep going. You have no option, anyway. In my case, I remained on a high through nearly four weeks of intensive operations, and I was only to feel tired after my own war had ended.

At this stage, the Argentinians had decided that the best means of getting supplies safely to their troops ashore was by parachuting them from Hercules or other transport aircraft. A landing on the damaged runway at Stanley by a heavy aircraft was difficult, though I believe it was done occasionally. But a Hercules would usually be escorted by two or more fighter aircraft as it approached the Islands. We were sent in to try and intercept any such aircraft heading towards the airfield or a parachute-dropping location nearby.

After bombarding overnight, on 9 May we took up a position about twelve miles south-west of Stanley, ready at dawn for any movement in the sky. Later that day, a Hercules and four escorting aircraft were detected by our radars as they closed on Stanley. They flew on into missile range, and all our systems were go. I was worried that the Hercules would detect us and turn away out of range and so decided to open fire at thirty-eight miles, close to the Sea Dart's maximum range. I fired one missile at the Hercules and a second at two Skyhawks flying in close formation. Both seemed to miss.

In my immediate report of the action, I said that I had failed to hit the targets. The Admiral must have been extremely disappointed, as of course was I, but he none the less sent a sympathetic reply and advised next time that I should wait to see the whites of the enemy's eyes before opening fire. He was quite right; I had been too eager and should have waited for just a few seconds more before engaging. However, *Broadsword* had been watching on her radar and had seen the second missile fly straight and true towards the Skyhawks. The two aircraft had then disappeared. They had either collided as they tried to avoid the missile or been knocked out of the sky when the missile exploded at the end of its flight. We had killed two birds with one stone.

Later on, still with *Broadsword* in support, my missile-guidance radar gained a fast-moving contact over the land. This contact had, in fact, been passed to me directly by data link from *Broadsword*, whose doppler radar was much more likely to detect this sort of target. I identified it as enemy and engaged with one missile at a range of thirteen miles. We scored a direct hit: the Puma troop-carrying helicopter blew up in a ball of fire and fell out of the sky, all on board being killed. I signalled a report of the action to the Admiral and in the final paragraph I added: 'I can confirm that the Argentinians do have whites to their eyes.' It was a ghoulish thing to say, but that's war for you.

It had been a successful day. After this, I believe, no transport aircraft came that far east again and certainly did not try and drop supplies over Stanley airfield. The enemy was now restricted to making parachute drops over a grass strip on the western side of West Falkland or supplying by sea, although this, too, had its risks: *Alacrity* had earlier engaged and destroyed a vessel bringing in supplies from the south and heading for Port Howard in Falkland Sound.

Able Seaman Richard Hopgood wrote later: 'This was another long day – the morning on the bridge followed by ten hours on the port gun direction platform. It was grey, with dark clouds, and cold. During the late afternoon or early evening a contact was spotted on the radar, and we heard the procedures for firing the Sea Dart coming over the gunnery speakers. We took cover as the missile came on the launcher and was fired. Once the smoke had disappeared, we headed to the bridge wing. I could see the trail of the missile heading off just to the port of the ship's head and over the land. Then it found its target, and the Puma exploded. We were over the moon. Five minutes earlier, we had been cold, bored and whingeing. Now we were shouting and cheering like our team had scored a vital goal in a football match. The rest of the watch went quickly and the boredom and cold, for a short time at least, had disappeared.'

But the day was not quite finished. A Harrier carrying out a high-level bombing of the airfield spotted a suspicious-looking surface vessel and contacted *Coventry*, which was controlling the aircraft, to ask whether we knew anything about it and whether there were any friendly ships in the vicinity. It was a surprise to me, but I told the pilot to investigate. He identified the vessel as the *Narwal*, a stern trawler flying the Argentinian flag, then asked me for instructions. We had some intelligence information on this vessel and were fairly certain it was up to no good, so I ordered the Harrier, 'Take it out.' He dropped a bomb on it and raked it with cannon fire. The bomb hit but did not explode, as it was armed for a high-level drop, but more than enough damage was done. The vessel stopped and the crew began to abandon ship.

The *Narwal* and its crew were duly captured by a boarding party put on the vessel by a Sea King helicopter. She later sank but not before we had been able to confirm that the ship had been involved in spying operations: there was an Argentinian officer on board with secret documents. Immediately afterwards, I was asked to explain my actions in ordering the attack as some thought initially that this might have been a genuinely neutral fishing vessel going about its innocent business. I breathed several sighs of relief when it was indeed proved to have been hostile and had been reporting the movements of the Carrier Battle Group back to mainland Argentina.

I had time to get another letter off to D on 11 May: 'I hope you still feel you are through the worst and you're able to bear the strain of me being involved in this war. I am sure you are being as brave as you can and I hope the children are a help rather than an extra worry. I am as fit as a fiddle and facing up to the whole situation well. We have been in quite a lot of action and we have been successful in our attacks. I am confident that we shall survive unharmed and that it won't be going on for much longer. A tumultuous homecoming is not far away.' I may have invariably commented on my rude health in my letters, but it was true all the same. There was no time to be ill, and it never occurred to me that I would be.

Buoyed up by our successes with Sea Dart missiles, I was keen to remain where I was, south-west of Stanley and, indeed, to move further west to have a better chance of intercepting the enemy's air supply lines as they approached West Falkland. However, I was ordered to leave the area and return to my

screening duties ahead of the Battle Group. *Glasgow* took over
from me on the Stanley gun line, bombarding overnight and
staying there next day to do battle with the enemy in the air.
Although I did not appreciate it at the time, I had been spared,
at least for the time being.

It was now 12 May and *Glasgow*, patrolling south of Stanley
in company with *Brilliant*, came under determined attack by
several Skyhawks. *Brilliant* was fully alert and shot down two
aircraft with her Sea Wolf missiles, while a third crashed into the
sea while trying to avoid a missile. A second wave came in and
this time *Brilliant*'s missile system suffered a technical hitch at a
crucial moment, rendering her all but defenceless, yet the two
bombs released in her direction bounced over the top of her and
landed in the water on the other side, causing no damage.
Glasgow was not so fortunate, however, as a 1,000-pound bomb
hit her amidships near the waterline and passed straight through
her hull and out the other side before exploding harmlessly
in the sea. Miraculously, there was not too much structural
damage, but *Glasgow* now had two large holes about three feet
across on either side of the ship and there was a considerable
amount of damage in the forward engine room.

The sea was not rough at the time, otherwise *Glasgow* would
surely have been lost. As it was, she did a marvellous job in
patching herself up and remaining afloat, but had to withdraw
to the east under the protection of the Battle Group for more
major repairs. She did not take any further part in front-line
work but continued to provide warning to the group of enemy
air activity. Eventually, she limped back slowly to the UK. Her
withdrawal was a great loss, since, of the Sea Dart-carrying
Type 42s, the entire Task Force was now left with only *Coventry*

to take the offensive to the enemy and provide control for the Harriers. Two more Type 42s, *Exeter* and *Cardiff*, were scheduled to join us but they were over a week away and the air threat remained very significant.

I reflected on how D's grandfather, John Luce, the captain of the light cruiser *Glasgow*, had had a similar narrow escape when his ship had been part of that British squadron involved in a surface action against the Germans off Coronel on the western coast of Chile in November 1914. The encounter had been a resounding defeat for the British, and *Glasgow* had been hit five times, the worst damage being caused by a 4.1-inch shell which left a six-foot-square hole in the hull on the waterline above her port propellers. However, she had lived to fight another day and had been present at the Battle of the Falklands a month later, when a British force including two battle cruisers decisively avenged the earlier defeat at Coronel.

Captain Luce had written in his report after Coronel: 'The conduct of the officers, petty officers and men throughout was certainly admirable. Under the trying circumstances of receiving a considerable volume of fire without being able to make an adequate return, perfect coolness and discipline prevailed . . . the gunlayers behaved exactly as at ordinary battle practice.' My own post-battle report was to say much the same.

The Battle of the Falklands had been fought in an area some sixty miles to the south-east of Stanley, not far from where the Carrier Battle Group was now operating. Then, in December 1914, it had been midsummer, whereas now we were approaching midwinter and facing the prospect of bad weather, something which would not be helpful to our troops, shortly to be fighting ashore. And how different it must have been in 1914.

The use of wireless was still in its infancy and there were no
deliveries of mail, so it must have been difficult to keep up
morale among the sailors, whose physical health and happiness
had to be maintained in cramped and harsh conditions. Coaling
had to be done every seven to ten days, and the bags had to be
filled by hand, hoisted on board by derricks and then carried on
wheelbarrows to be discharged down a variety of small hatches
on the deck. Everybody and everything was covered in a fine
black dust: it was often difficult to distinguish one face from
another. Furthermore, the ships were poorly ventilated, so very
uncomfortable in warm weather, and home to millions of cock-
roaches. Meals brought little consolation either, consisting as
they did mainly of corned beef, rice and mouldy bread. Both
conditions and communications were, of course, very different
in *Coventry* in 1982, and this made things much easier for me
than they had been for John Luce.

At the day's end on 14 May, I wrote a letter home which
included news of my actions against the patrol vessels and the
helicopter. These short moments snatched for letter-writing
were very precious and I found them calming. 'Just got three
letters from you – marvellous. So relieved to hear you are all
remaining well and calm. Letter from my mother saying you are
all being wonderful and Miranda especially helpful and understanding – and looking so pretty with gorgeous liquid brown
eyes like Devon pools. Lovely to hear that. I am fine and coping well – and the ship's company magnificent. Don't worry, I
am well up to the hectic routine. Rough weather and little sleep
I take well in my stride.'

My mother's mention of Devon pools referred to a stretch of
the River Teign above Chagford, close to where my grand-

parents lived. As a small child, when my father was away at sea, I often stayed with my grandparents, along with my mother, brother and two sisters. We children frequently ran down the steeply sloping lawns to our favourite spots by the river where we either swam in the still pools or clambered over the large, moss-covered boulders which littered the river bed, leaping from one to another. Those deep brown pools, with their golden shingle which shone through to the surface in the sunlight, were magical, and they perfectly evoked Miranda's eyes.

I duly enclosed with my letter a note to Miranda and Alice which consisted mainly of one of my sketches of *Coventry* firing missiles at the enemy. I have always enjoyed drawing and so it must have given me a moment of relaxation at the end of another long day, but looking back it does seem rather unchivalrous to have glorified and made light of these actions involving such loss of life. There again, perhaps I was just trying to reassure my young daughters by making the war sound fun rather than dangerous. If I was, though, I was deluding both them and myself.

CHAPTER 7

UNDER PRESSURE

After the attack on *Glasgow*, it was decided that no more bombardments would take place in daylight; it was now imperative to preserve our limited resources and not to take undue risks. But we had to keep inflicting as much damage as possible to weaken the enemy so as to make an amphibious landing possible: some risks had to be taken or we would never win. Besides, we were in a race against time to avoid the worsening weather and now had only seventeen Harriers. Soon, we would lose two more: one would be shot down by ground fire and the other blown up just after take-off, killing the pilot.

We were feeling the strain. We had been fighting a fairly intense war for nearly two weeks, and our days were long as we had to be constantly alert and ready for action from dawn until dusk. Darkness brought no respite, for it was then we often had to dash back to the Carrier Battle Group to replenish our fuel and ammunition. This was hard work, requiring much manpower to prepare and carry out these evolutions safely and speedily. It was a navigational and ship-handling nightmare to find your way on a dark night in bad weather to your designated tanker among a concentrated mass of ships, none of which were burning navigation lights or communicating on voice circuits. This policy of ships being darkened and keeping radio silence was intended to avoid giving away the position of the Battle Group to the enemy, but for us it made a difficult business even more so. The approach to find the tanker or stores ship was hardly helped by the bridge radar picture, which showed only a mass of bright blips all over the screen, like measles, every one of them the same size. Which one did you go for? Eventually, a red flashing light would become a distant, ghostly shape and you knew you had identified the right vessel. *Coventry* was fortunate to have had in Lieutenant Tim Harris a very competent and level-headed navigating officer, and it was always a great relief to be steaming safely in the replenishing position alongside the ship which had been expecting us.

The submarine threat, real or imagined, remained a constant anxiety, although when night came and we had survived attacks from the air, we felt we could relax, even if only a little. I assumed my officers and sailors must be getting very tired but they did seem to be surprisingly good-humoured, alert and fit. A number of men in the warfare team, who had to look for long periods at bright displays in the subdued lighting of the operations room, began to get eye-strain or conjunctivitis, and increasingly that became a problem, although they were treatable. The colours of the electronically generated graphics on the displays and plots became quite hard on the eyes after a time. Even so, people bore up remarkably well and morale remained high.

Lieutenant Ray Adams, the communications officer, was

interviewed not long after the conflict and asked what it was like being at war. He said it was just like normal exercising: you were only doing what you had practised so often in peacetime. In this respect, he was right — it was not difficult to be at war, such had been the rigour and discipline of our training. We would certainly not have been able to remain so cheerful and confident had it not been so thorough and realistic. For my part, I always tried to inject some good news into my nightly broadcasts to the ship's company, even though there may not have been much. I could sense these broadcasts meant a great deal to people and they had to be carefully planned: I had to combine humour, hope and encouragement, as well as report on how the war was going. This was not easy, especially on the occasion when two of our warships had just been sunk not far from us. But it was crucial that I shared as much information as I could and took everyone into my confidence: we were, after all, a team which depended on each other for our lives.

During action stations, I employed the senior weapons engineer officer, Commander Geoffrey Lane, in the operations room to inform key personnel in the weapons and engineering departments and the damage-control headquarters about what was happening: his running commentaries on the internal communication lines to these people in more remote parts of the ship always ensured they were kept abreast of developments and ready to respond rapidly to any emergencies, defects or damage. I also made the relevant classified signals, including intelligence, available to all the heads of departments so they were aware of what the Task Force as a whole was doing and the various missions that were being undertaken. It was important to include those not directly involved in conducting the fighting; again, it helped to maintain morale and it meant everyone was always prepared for whatever action might be required.

In the absence of a chaplain on board, I upheld the naval tradition of taking church services on Sundays and these, not surprisingly, became rather better attended than usual. I would not say that I am especially religious, but I have always believed in a God and a life for us all in some form after death. It is a rather simple faith, I have to admit, but I have invariably gained strength at difficult moments from believing that there is a superior power or being of some kind, and I have never liked to think that death is absolutely final. I certainly thought it was important to hold services on board, especially at this time, and I took trouble to select the hymns, lesson and prayers. In the Naval Prayer we exhorted 'the Eternal Lord God to protect us from the dangers of the sea and the violence of the enemy', while the hymn 'Eternal Father, Strong to Save' was a cry for 'those in peril on the sea'. Both had a startling relevance and were recited or sung with great conviction and not a few lumps in the throat.

I needed to maintain quite a stiff upper lip on these occasions. I even read the prayer which the petty officer had earlier presented me with on the bridge. It was a Catholic imprecation to St Joseph, patron of departing souls, and it began: 'Oh, St Joseph whose protection is so strong, so great, so prompt before the throne of God, I place in you all my interests and desires . . . assist me by your powerful intercession . . . pray for me.' On the back of the prayer were the words: 'Whoever shall read this prayer or hear it, or keep it about themselves, shall never die a sudden death, or be drowned. Neither shall they fall into the hands of the enemy or be overpowered in battle. This prayer was discovered in 50 AD and it has never been known to fail.'

Later, another copy of this prayer appeared on my desk in my cabin, this time typed on a card. Nothing was said but I knew who had left it there and why. And even though I thought no more about it, I kept the prayer on me for the rest of the war.

In the early days particularly, it was wonderful to get letters from home and to know that ours were also getting back. I must have asked my wife for some more lapsang souchong tea at some point, which seems rather frivolous now. But I always used to have a cup of this tea, then my favourite, on the bridge with a slice of toast and Marmite at about 4 p.m, often brought to me by Steward Steve Hale. Certain routines are well worth preserving if at all possible when everything about you is uncertain, just as there is nothing better than to assume an air of normality when there is none anywhere else. To my delight, with D's next letter came a packet of my tea, both delivered as usual by helicopter. It was not a bad service, all considered, and in its own small way it illustrated just how astonishing was the logistical organization of this whole operation.

As time went on, though, I found it harder to open letters from home. I had, of course, written to D frequently since leaving Gibraltar, but before the war started in earnest I had written what I then thought might well be my last letter for the duration. It had been an upbeat one. I had received a similarly cheerful one from D at about the same time, full of encouragement and pride and, even more importantly, saying all was well at home and that the girls were in good spirits and doing well at school. D had added that all our friends were being supportive and the *Coventry* wives and girlfriends were being looked after and bearing up well. This was the memory I wanted to hold on to – that of a happy situation at home. But as the war became more hectic and hazardous and we began to suffer losses, I feared to get a letter which might express some unhappiness or anxiety. For D to write of her worries would be entirely understandable, but equally, I would not want to read about them as I went into battle.

More than almost anything else, I needed contentment of mind. I had to put thoughts of family and home determinedly out of my mind; even family photographs in my cabin had to be put away. I did open my letters, of course, but increasingly I found that they became an emotional distraction and so I could not dwell on them. Instead, I would put them aside, not always read in their entirety, and I would go out and around the ship to concentrate once more on the war. Once I had wrenched myself away from my letters and thoughts of those I loved at home, it always cheered me up to talk to my officers and sailors. If I had not done this, I think I might have been caught at a moment of weakness, with all my defences down. I now knew what putting on a brave face really meant, and that in war it was a very necessary thing to do.

I also began to notice how a few members of the ship's company were beginning to feel the strain, although usually all that was needed was a little timely encouragement to put them right again. The most obvious symptom of fear or anxiety was that someone seemed unusually subdued and preoccupied, and this was especially noticeable among those who were normally outgoing. I think it was easier sometimes for the younger members of the ship's company to remain strong and fearless, since as a rule they had fewer family responsibilities. Those with wives and children were inevitably more affected by the dangers. I observed, too, how those with watch-keeping duties, and they were the majority, found the life easier to bear because they were being kept very busy and so had less time to dwell on potential dangers or disasters. The first lieutenant, whose duties meant that he did not keep a watch, certainly became a little quieter.

Lieutenant-Commander Rob Hamilton, *Coventry*'s marine engineer officer, had also noticed changes in some people quite early on, well before the start of hostilities: they were becoming quieter and less effective at their jobs just at a time when everyone else was becoming more efficient and rising to the challenge. He believed they were suffering from battle stress, even though we were not yet at war. Officers as well as ratings were affected and, as they always do, people covered for each other. All that could be done to help, Rob Hamilton concluded, was to offer quiet encouragement and support and to keep a careful eye on the weaker members of any team. The important thing was always to identify those who had been adversely affected and to make absolutely sure they did not fall short or become careless in their work, thereby causing danger to others or the ship. Looking back, he recorded that only a very few individuals had suffered in this way and performed less well.

Despite everything, laughter was never far away. In particular, the bridge watch-keepers were a close-knit team who remained positive throughout. Yeoman of Signals David Nuttall and Radio Supervisor Sam MacFarlane, both of whom bore a tremendous workload and responsibility as they sent, processed and distributed a mass of incoming signals, amused themselves and many around them by keeping a tally of the aircraft shot down on the communication office door in the main passageway. 'The score's on the doors!' – mimicking Bruce Forsyth's catchphrase in the television show *The Generation Game* – was always the cry as the latest kill was chalked up for everyone to see.

Sitting on the edge of my bunk early one morning, I found myself contemplating a completely flat chest with every rib showing through my lean frame. It gave me quite a shock: I looked like a prisoner of war. I was actually very fit, though, and the constant need to proceed up and down ladders and along moving decks had probably given me a far better workout than any gymnasium ashore. We ate quite well, even if it was invariably rather more of the same and kept very simple in order to ease the burden on the chefs. The officers ate the same as the ship's company; there were no frills or fancy foods for the wardroom or for me as there might have been in peacetime. Like everyone else, I winced slightly at the prospect of another potmess which, as its name would suggest, was just that – the naval equivalent of a poor man's goulash. I reckoned that my loss of weight was largely due to the nervous energy I had expended – living on the edge, as it were. I never compared notes with anyone else but I am sure we all slimmed down considerably during the conflict. I certainly wish I could see more of my ribs now.

In the meantime, the SAS had hatched a plan to take out the Exocet-carrying Super Étendard aircraft on the ground in southern Argentina. I read about the mission, which was to take place a day or two before our troops were due to land, with some excitement and, like everyone else, I was desperate for it to succeed. We duly escorted *Invincible* part of the way as she steamed south and west of the Falkland Islands in order to get as close as she dared to the mainland before launching a Sea King helicopter with the SAS team on board. The helicopter would land on a lake in friendly territory in southern Chile near the border with Argentina, whereupon it would be sunk to hide all evidence of its arrival. The team would lie low ashore for two days before making their way to the relevant air base or bases and destroying the Étendards.

It all looked relatively straightforward on paper and the instructions to the SAS team on how to get back after the mission read simply: 'You are on your own.' Unfortunately, the helicopter, which was flying at the extreme limit of its range, probably just ran out of fuel and had to crash-land on terra firma. Attempts were made to burn the machine but it was inevitably discovered, and the Argentinians promptly doubled up security on their airfields. Everyone involved eventually returned safely, but the mission's failure was a bitter blow as the Exocet would now remain a threat to the very end. To make matters worse, the SAS suffered a terrible loss shortly afterwards when a helicopter carrying a large number of its members crashed into the sea: twenty-two of the thirty SAS men on board were killed.

But if we greatly feared the Exocet, then the Argentinians must have been terrified of the Harrier with its two Sidewinder infra-red homing air-to-air missiles, which proved to be very reliable and unerringly accurate. The operational readiness of the aircraft itself was extremely high, reflecting both the skill of the aircrew and technicians involved and the standards they achieved in maintenance and repair. (At one time *Hermes* had twelve Harriers airborne out of her total of fourteen and the last two were at five minutes' notice on deck.) This fine record was in turn a tribute to the design of the aircraft, which was to prove both very robust and remarkably manoeuvrable in combat, capable of out-flying much faster and more sophisticated enemy fighters. All this, combined with the skill of the pilots themselves and the quality of their training, made the aircraft a real winner.

The superb reliability of the Harrier was, however, in stark contrast to that of the weapons and equipment in our ships. At least, that was my experience. *Coventry* always required a great deal of skill and ingenuity on the part of her technicians and maintenance personnel to keep her fully operational and fighting fit. Initiative and courage were often needed too: once, a chief petty officer took it upon himself to climb to the top of the mainmast in the middle of an air attack to repair a defective radar aerial.

In 1982, *Coventry* was some three years old and so had accumulated three years' worth of defects. These had been building up slowly, and by no means all had been dealt with, largely on account of a lack of spare parts. Indeed, there had been a general concern in the Navy about the various economies recently imposed on the service and the effect this might have on the supply of certain important stores and spares for the ships. In *Coventry*'s case, the upshot was that everything seemed to go wrong in the ship, and it did so just before the start of hostilities.

At one time, we had a serious steering-gear failure and had to manoeuvre and keep station on other ships either using a hand pump or the ship's engines. We had a series of other mechanical problems as well as a nasty contamination in the fuel tanks. The marine engineers had their work cut out to rectify all these problems, but everything was remedied just in time. Much to our relief, the main engines, which consisted of four gas turbines, remained very reliable. For economical cruising, the ship was driven by two Tyne gas turbines, but when speed was required, the two Olympus engines were started and all four engines together could propel the ship up to 30 knots very quickly. This revolutionary arrangement in propulsion machinery, jointly pioneered by the Royal Navy and Rolls-Royce, had set a world-wide course for change, and today every major navy has gas turbine-powered ships.

The Rolls-Royce Olympus engines, the same as those fitted in Concorde, were extremely powerful and provided both speed and acceleration. In the past, destroyers had always been designed with these characteristics, and in the Second World War they had often been able to escape being hit when in open water. My own instinct, therefore, was always to use maximum power and speed during air attacks so I could, if necessary, alter course very rapidly. But this would rather depend upon my not being in close company with another ship – a ship that I would not be able to see from the operations room. A modern destroyer such as *Coventry* was intended to be fought blind while its radars tracked an enemy some distance away. And however much I might have wanted to be on the bridge during an attack, this was not my place. I had to have control over the ship's main weapon systems, and since these could only be fired from the operations room, that was where I had to remain. In this sense, I always rather felt I was fighting with my hands tied behind my back.

A good turn of speed was useful in other situations as well – for example, whenever we went to replenish from a tanker in the main group of ships some distance to the east of the Falklands and then had to return as quickly as we could to our front-line position near the Islands, ready to counter the air threat. All the ship's main machinery and controls were, in fact, well-proven aircraft technology. Rather than the traditional helm situated in a wheelhouse and manned by a strong-armed sailor who wrestled with the wheel in rough weather, we had a joystick control on the bridge. This had the lightest of touches and enabled the ship to be steered accurately in all weathers. Moreover, you could switch to automatic and the control system would steer the ship for you – and probably with greater accuracy than a quartermaster whose concentration might be wavering.

We were now nearing the end of the third week in May and moving towards the final, critical phase of the war – preparing for the landings and the subsequent land battle. The Amphibious Task Group led by Commodore Michael Clapp, Royal Navy, and the Landing Force Group commanded by Brigadier Julian Thompson, Royal Marines, were not far away and poised to head towards the Falklands as soon as the air threat became acceptable and the date for the landings had been decided. The means of landing the troops and equipment was provided by the specialist ships of the Amphibious Task Group, namely the assault ships *Fearless* and *Intrepid* and the five RFA landing ships of the Sir Lancelot class. The Landing Force consisted mainly of three Royal Marine Commandos and two Battalions of the Parachute Regiment, with all their heavy equipment and vehicles, transported in the large P&O cruise ship *Canberra*, the North Sea ferry *Norland*, the P&O ferry *Elk*, the Townsend Thoresen ship *Europic Ferry*, all requisitioned for this purpose, and RFA *Stromness*. The force was completed by several frigate and destroyer escorts.

This was perhaps the most demanding and dangerous period as we continued to battle for dominance of the skies around the Islands. And, as ever, there was the weather to worry about. It was about this time, when we were on our way to take up a position to the north-west of West Falkland, that *Coventry* detected a Argentinian Boeing surveillance aircraft flying over the Islands which presented an ideal target for our Sea Dart missiles. We had the system all ready to go and waited until it came into range. It seemed too good to be true, and the excitement was almost unbearable. Then the computer gave me the green light and I gave the order to fire. Nothing happened. I felt sick with anger and frustration, and my mood was not improved when I learnt that the flash doors through which the missile passed on to the launcher had temporarily jammed shut and that as a result the whole system had switched off. We had missed a golden opportunity to deliver a massive blow to the enemy's surveillance capability – and probably to Galtieri himself, whose personal aeroplane I believe it was. The problem was solved by a sailor going on to the upper deck with a large hammer to break away accumulations of salt and straighten out the hatch which had been damaged by buffeting from heavy seas. But it was too late. The Boeing, sensing our presence, turned and made for home. It was difficult to get over this failure: I could only hope that, once frightened, the Boeing would stay away, although it was little consolation to learn later that it probably did just that.

The Battle Group's own airborne surveillance was extremely limited and we badly needed long-range aircraft with good surface search radar to give us a reliable picture of any enemy movement at sea. We still could not be sure that all elements of the Argentinian Navy had been confined to their territorial waters or bases. Our submarines could not easily track all the comings and goings of enemy shipping, especially in shallow coastal waters, and the Sea King helicopters did not have either sufficient endurance or the best radar for this purpose. It was a genuine weakness, but the RAF eventually managed somehow to get an in-flight-refuelled Nimrod aircraft from Ascension down to our area of operations to scour the ocean before the vital heavy ships of the Amphibious Task Group and Landing Force neared the Islands. It was this crucial piece of surveillance that gave the all-clear as far as the surface threat was concerned.

Meanwhile, 8,000 miles away in Petersfield, D and the children had been writing on 15 May. Alice's letter was, as ever, full of fond hope: 'Darling Daddy, I dreamt that you came back in the middle of the night and brought some presents. One was a typewriter for Miranda, and one was a Mickey Mouse and Donald Duck puppet for me, and for Mummy a pet kitten and also a lovely plant. I hope you come back soon. Much love, Alice your lovely daughter.'

Miranda's was, after its fashion, more informative, although it did contain one glaring misspelling: 'Mummy has just developed your photographs that you sent us. They are very nice, and some of them go back to last summer. I have lost the key to the summer house and the door won't shut. In the night the door slammed and all the glass came out. In one of the photographs you were wearing white shorts and had very knobely knees! Mummy had three ladies to supper and we handed round drinks and crisps, and shared a packet between Alice and I. Much love from Miranda.'

Inevitably, D's own letter was rather more emotional, and it was probably just as well that I did not receive it until I was on my way home: 'It was so wonderful to get the letters from you today – written on 26 and 28 April. Heaven knows when this will reach you. Every time I write I always pray by the time you get the letter you will have turned round and be on your way home again. Yesterday Chris Morgan [a naval friend] looked in for tea, which was a very good moment as I'd just heard that a Type 42 had had a bomb dropped through it and he could tell me it was not *Coventry*. But had it been a day earlier it could have been you – as you were in that area. Chris also told me how well *Coventry* was doing – and entirely due to you, I've no doubt!

'Your nerves must be torn to shreds inside you – although I'm sure you never show it. Everyone is very aware of the tremendous strain on you all of fighting in very rough seas, and having to be constantly on the alert. How you ever sleep at all I can't think. Perhaps it's like the last war when people just kept going while they had to – and then collapsed totally when they got home.

'Last night I had Elizabeth Gotto, Wendy Larken and Sheila Balfour [all naval wives] to supper, which was a great success. Looking around the table, I thought suddenly how much older we all looked. Certainly, I've got many more grey hairs since the Falkland crisis began – but hopefully the years will fall away when you return. Wendy and I sat and talked the other day about how we felt we would react if we heard either *Coventry* or *Fearless* had been sunk, and you weren't coming home. It's something in the back of all our minds – but so horrific that one hardly dares contemplate it.

'It was good to talk about it. We both felt that despite the agony and the grief, we would simply keep going on through life in the same way – for the sake of the children – and because there is no other way to be. So don't ever worry that I wouldn't be able to cope – I know I would – and at least I would go through the rest of life remembering a perfect marriage and a wonderful husband – and nothing could ever take that away. Having said all that, I know I will see you steam into Portsmouth harbour in a few months' time – I just wanted to put your mind at rest over that particular subject.

'I have Cornwall firmly fixed in my mind and I know you will be home for it. And then we must have a week alone somewhere really relaxing and peaceful. The thought of that – and how much I love you – keeps me going, so never worry about us.'

CHAPTER 8

TOUCH AND GO

With *Sheffield* sunk and *Glasgow* put out of action, *Coventry* now shouldered more of the hazardous tasks. If we were not on a protective screen ahead of the carriers, we were deployed mainly to the north of West Falkland in company with *Broadsword*, armed with her highly effective Sea Wolf missile system. We were there to fight off the incoming air raids with Harriers and Sea Dart missiles, while being protected by *Broadsword*. Although it was not spelt out in as many words, it was clear to me that we had to draw the enemy fire towards us and away from the landing zone of San Carlos Water at the northern end of Falkland Sound, and that we were to be sacrificed if necessary. Although every ship involved in the war had drawn a short straw, ours, I think, was the shortest. During the next few days *Coventry* would be in the front line against an enemy hell-bent on preventing a landing and advance on Stanley.

There is ample precedent in Royal Naval history where individual ships have been deliberately risked or sacrificed to enable other more important units to survive. A classic example was that of HMS *Jervis Bay* in November 1940, when she was the sole escort of a convoy of thirty-seven ships homeward-bound from Halifax, Nova Scotia. The Admiralty received an alarming signal that the convoy was being attacked by the German pocket battleship *Admiral Scheer*, not known until then to have broken out into the North Atlantic. The 14,000-ton *Jervis Bay*, commanded by Captain Fogarty Fegen, RN, was one of a number of weakly armed and vulnerable ex-liners converted for the Royal Navy to make up the shortfall in heavy ships and cruisers. Captain Fegen did not hesitate to close and open fire on *Admiral Scheer*, old six-inch guns against eleven-inch, thin plating against thick armour, while signalling the convoy to disperse. Within twenty minutes *Jervis Bay*, a shattered hulk with her bridge on fire, had capsized, taking her captain with her. Fegen's self-sacrifice had won enough time for all but five ships of the convoy to escape. He was awarded a posthumous Victoria Cross.

My letter to D of 16 May gave both a glimpse of my life at sea and my generally confident mood: 'Do hope you are coping with the whole situation, but it must be very difficult. I am really in very good shape and my sailors are standing up to the pace very well. We have had some difficult moments but I am sure that *Coventry* will survive unharmed. The news of *Sheffield* must have been an awful shock for you, but there is little chance of that being repeated. You will be glad to hear it's not always rough down here. Today is a lovely calm day, though very cold. When I get the chance, the first lieutenant takes command of the ship overnight and I can catch up with some sleep. So I manage to keep myself reasonably fresh and alert for the busy moments.

I dare say I am ageing rapidly and hair continues to fall out, so I hope you will recognize me when I get home. I miss the green fields and trees of England and can't wait to see the garden.'

In most respects, the letter was truthful. I was in good shape and so busy and concentrated, as well as high on adrenalin, that I no longer felt any fear. Life was to a large extent exciting, exhilarating even, and there was no question of being anything other than strong and calm at all times. The officers, the sailors watch-keeping on the bridge and those in the operations room with whom I rubbed shoulders frequently, all helped me keep going. I felt protective towards them, I cared for them, and I felt part of a team which did as much to inspire me as, I hoped, I did to inspire them.

D-Day had now been set for 21 May and it was not long before the mass of shipping, with all our troops, their weapons and equipment, appeared over the horizon. For a few hours, the Amphibious Task Group and the Landing Force Group joined up with the Carrier Battle Group, exchanging signals, receiving vital stores and transferring personnel. It was an awe-inspiring sight, and this assembly of over one hundred ships summed up just what was at stake for us all. These three powerful groups made up the entire Task Force, complete and together for the first time, and were poised to embark on the most perilous phase of the campaign: the largest British amphibious operation since the Second World War and, to my mind, probably one of the riskiest. I beckoned to one or two officers and ratings on the bridge to have a good look before the reducing visibility obscured the sight of this vast armada. A broadcast to the ship's company alerted others below who came up on deck to see for themselves.

Among the new arrivals with the Amphibious Force were two Type 42s, *Exeter* and *Cardiff*, commanded by Captain Hugh Balfour and Captain Mike Harris respectively. Others included the frigate *Argonaut* (Captain Kit Layman) and the Type 21 frigates *Ardent* (Commander Alan West) and *Antelope* (Commander Nick Tobin). However, I never caught sight of these ships as our differing roles kept us apart. The old hands *Antrim*, *Plymouth*, *Yarmouth*, *Brilliant* and *Broadsword* had, along with *Argonaut* and *Ardent*, the unenviable task of escorting the amphibious ships into Falkland Sound under threat of attack by submarine and aircraft. *Fearless* (Captain Jeremy Larken) and *Intrepid* (Captain Peter Dingemans), the twin landing assault ships, were the spearhead of the force, followed closely by the *Canberra*, *Norland* and *Stromness*. Five RFA landing ships and *Fort Austin* completed this highly specialized fleet.

Alacrity had been ordered to pass, from the south, northwards through the entrance to the Sound a day or two before the arrival of the main force to check whether any mines had been laid. On the face of it, it did seem rather foolhardy to use an expensive frigate as a minesweeper when she would only be able to confirm the presence of mines after an explosion under her hull, but at this time we had no other means of detecting or sweeping mines. There had, however, been no evidence of mine-laying in this area and so the risks were not considered high. When Commander Chris Craig was told of this hazardous mission by the Admiral, he immediately sensed its significance and volunteered to make several passes with *Alacrity* through the northern approaches to the Sound. This was a brave gesture and just what Sandy Woodward had in mind.

As it was, all turned out well and the passage through to San

Carlos Water was found to be clear of hazards. But there remained the possibility of attacks by submarines and my old fear returned: it looked all too easy for the enemy to position his submarines off the entrance to the Sound and pick off the heavy ships as they passed through – and such an action alone would probably have won the war for the Argentinians. Our anti-submarine frigate escorts were specifically instructed to search for submarine contacts throughout the landing phase, but mercifully there were none.

I managed to sound quite upbeat in a letter to D of 20 May: 'I remain very well and on top of all my responsibilities. I speak to the ship's company every evening and try and encourage them and keep up their morale. It's a hard life for them at the moment. I think the worst will be over in about a week with any luck. I must tell them tonight that they are all my heroes – because they really are. I couldn't wish for a better ship's company in these difficult times. *Coventry* is doing well and we have done our fair share of work against the enemy. Always touching wood, we seem to have got over our machinery problems and all our weapons are on top line. Nor have we suffered any action damage. The thought of being home is paradise. There are more ships on the way which hopefully will relieve those of us who have been here from the very start – so home can't be too far away.' This, as it turned out, was to be the last letter I wrote from *Coventry*. And I did indeed tell my crew that they were heroes that night and how they would be welcomed as such when they got home.

The Amphibious Task Group and Landing Force went into Falkland Sound overnight under cover of darkness on 20/21 May. The first wave of amphibious units landed on the beaches of San Carlos at 4.30 a.m. local time and the second at first light. The anticipated air threat did not materialize until two and a half hours after sunrise, by which time some 3,000 troops and stores had been successfully got ashore. By the end of the day, a further 2,000 troops had been safely landed. The outcome of the war would now depend on securing the beachhead from which the troops could advance and fight, and the setting up of Rapier anti-aircraft missile batteries on the higher ground above the beaches was therefore a priority. Everyone, whether ashore or afloat, was about to be tested to their limits.

As the waves of air attacks began, the Harriers did their best to wreak havoc among the enemy in order to protect the large group of vulnerable ships in the Sound. *Brilliant* took on the task of directing the Harriers and performed magnificently: a large number of kills against Skyhawks and Daggers were achieved, although some attacks on the frigate escorts could not be prevented. I was a bystander to this action as I had been summoned back to the Carrier Battle Group for screening duties since an Exocet attack on the carriers was thought likely. But I listened to the voices of the warfare officers in the ships being attacked as they strove to fight off their attackers. There was desperation in those voices as *Ardent* was being hit. Only when night came was there any respite, and *Ardent* was so badly damaged she eventually sank with the loss of twenty-two lives.

Argonaut was seriously damaged by bombs and had to be towed to a creek for repairs. The bombs had failed to go off, though, and were eventually defused. Similarly, *Antrim* was badly damaged by an unexploded bomb but she eventually recovered. Several of the other escorts suffered some damage from cannon fire and shrapnel; only *Plymouth* and *Yarmouth* came through unscathed. It had been a frantic day and it did not bode well: the enemy air force was clearly intent on throwing everything at us and was prepared both to take on the Harriers and risk the threat from our ships' missiles. Unfortunately, the shore-based Rapier missiles, perhaps affected by the long sea passage, seemed to be taking an age to get functioning effectively. It was tragic that the warships had to suffer so much, but exposing them was a deliberate tactic, for it was better that they were the targets rather than the valuable amphibious units with troops and equipment on board. The total killed in them on D-Day was twenty-seven.

Commodore Michael Clapp, who masterminded the amphibious landings and flew the broad pennant of Commodore Amphibious Warfare in *Fearless*, later wrote in his book, *Amphibious Assault Falklands*: 'It was not luck that the Argentinian pilots attacked the warships and not the landing ships. We had lots of time to think about it and the whole approach to the landings had been a threat-reduction exercise. The warships were placed so that the Argentinians had to fly close to them to get at the amphibious ships. Guns of every calibre were pressed into service and an enormous amount of tracer was fired to make the pilots twist and turn and to make it impossible for them to aim accurately.'

Miraculously, *Canberra* remained unharmed. After successfully disembarking the troops in her, she slid quietly out overnight and retreated to safe waters. It seems astonishing that this great ship, still painted in the white livery of P&O, could have steamed into 'Bomb Alley', as it became known, and stayed there in broad daylight and in full view of a large number of determined bomber pilots who were carrying out wave after wave of savage air attacks. Her escape was largely due to the positioning of the escorts and to her being anchored close to the hills surrounding San Carlos Water. This prevented aircraft from getting a long enough run in to the target for a viable bomb release. I believe the enthusiastic and daring Captain Christopher Burne, the senior Royal Navy officer in the 'Great White Whale', as *Canberra* was nicknamed, did much to calm down and encourage the liner's master when he was given the task of taking her into these treacherous waters. After all, this was not what he had joined P&O to do.

We were now ordered to join *Broadsword* in an area to the north and west of the Sound and we were to remain with her for the rest of our time. The aim was to act as a missile trap – to intercept aircraft as they made their landfalls to the west of the Islands before they could drop their bombs on the ships in the Sound. Although we could see the enemy aircraft on radar soon after they took off from their mainland bases over two hundred miles away, when they descended to low level on nearing the Islands we invariably lost them completely. They cleverly flew low over the land following the contours of the hills and were absorbed by the land clutter on our radar displays. We then became extremely vulnerable to surprise low-level attacks which our Sea Dart missile system was not designed to cope with. Frustratingly, too, we detected some aircraft approaching the Islands which then skirted around and outside our missile range before landing on the grass airstrip on West Falkland. After dropping off their supplies, they flew straight for home.

I suggested in a signal to Sandy Woodward that *Coventry* should operate alone much further to the west by the Jason Islands, where, unhindered by land, I could engage the aircraft before they came down to low level. But he did not agree as he thought it too risky and, if the ship got hit, he would not be able to come to my rescue. It would also be beyond the range of the Harriers. I had to agree it was risky but I reckoned it was worth a try: I thought I could hit and run among these islands and remain hidden.

With hindsight, though, I could see the importance of remaining where I was so as to be able to communicate with the ships in the Sound on secure short-range frequencies to warn them of developing air raids. For this reason, I had to remain no further than fifteen miles north of the Falklands in order to keep in contact and provide air warning and moral support to the ships and the troops consolidating ashore. If I had been operating some distance away, I would have had to rely on high-frequency long-range communications, which were susceptible to eavesdropping and jamming by the enemy.

I struck up a good working relationship with Bill Canning in *Broadsword* who was the senior officer tasked to provide protection for me with his ship's Sea Wolf missiles. Unlike our Sea Darts, these missiles were very short-range and designed to protect the ship itself from air attack, and so *Broadsword* had to keep close to *Coventry* if she was to be able to reach any target heading towards us. She would, therefore, try and position herself between us and the attacking aircraft. It all sounded fairly straightforward, but I could see the potential for difficulties. For reasons I have already discussed, it was going to be hard enough to manoeuvre in close company in the frantic moments of an air attack from one direction. But it was going to be even harder if we ever found ourselves under attack from aircraft coming at us from different directions, since then our

Coventry viewed from *Broadsword* as the two ships patrol on 25 May 1982
(R.W. Bell-Davies and C.M. Pickering)

Two Argentinian Skyhawks (circled) attack at low level and high speed: the shell splashes
are from defensive fire and the aircraft's cannon fire *(R.W. Bell-Davies and C.M. Pickering)*

The first bomb hits *Coventry* *(R.W. Bell-Davies and C.M. Pickering)*

The stricken ship, having lost all power after the attack *(R.W. Bell-Davies and C.M. Pickering)*

FROM TOP TO BOTTOM: Within minutes of being hit, *Coventry* starts to settle in the water. Life-rafts are launched from the destroyer, despite her ever-increasing list to port

(R.W. Bell-Davies and C.M. Pickering)

TOP: The view from a life-raft: the netting and ropes have been let down the side to facilitate escape *(M. Dilucia and M. Pattison)*

CENTRE: A Sea King helicopter makes a final search for survivors *(R.W. Bell-Davies and C.M. Pickering)*

BOTTOM: *Coventry* is by now completely inverted, with only the base of her hull and propellers showing above the surface. This is the last view her captain and crew would have of her *(R.W. Bell-Davies and C.M. Pickering)*

two ships were going to have to manoeuvre with absolutely split-second timing to give us both any chance of bringing our very different weapon systems to bear.

My instinct to increase speed when under attack would, of course, make it all the more difficult for *Broadsword* to get into the right position. Consequently, Bill Canning and I agreed that *Coventry* would be free to manoeuvre as required for firing Sea Dart but would not increase speed. This would make it easier for *Broadsword* to use her own speed advantage to position herself and give Sea Wolf a clear view of any approaching enemy aircraft. In fact, in the last conversation I had with Bill Canning, he simply said, 'Don't worry, David. You manoeuvre as you wish and I will keep out of your way.' Bill was always so calm, sensible and reassuring, and I felt there was an excellent understanding between us. The thing we most wanted to avoid was getting in each other's way as we reacted in the heat of the moment. *Coventry*'s radars were invariably looking for aircraft at longer ranges and so *Broadsword*, being close to us, could not be seen in the radar groundwave. It was a considerable relief, therefore, for us to know that *Broadsword* would take on the responsibility of keeping clear of us and manoeuvring as necessary to protect us.

As it was, my own apprehensions on this score were shared by others. After the war, the first lieutenant of *Brilliant*, Lee Hulme, an experienced aircraft controller who was responsible for the successes against the earlier air raids over the Sound, wrote to me: 'We were very aware of your exploits when operating with our sister ship *Broadsword* and in agreement with your signalled comments on the weakness involved in this method of operation when close to land.' He had had exactly the same experience of operating with the combination of long-range Sea Dart and short-range Sea Wolf ships – one that had, of course, eventually resulted in *Glasgow* being bombed and damaged. *Coventry*, unfortunately, was not to escape so lightly.

None the less, we settled into a routine, patrolling along an east/west line, with *Broadsword* keeping station about half a mile astern, ready for anything. Before each alteration of course, I would signal my intentions to *Broadsword* and give the new direction. As ever, the end of each day brought a huge sense of relief. We only ever saw our friendly forces to the east of the Islands when we refuelled or took on ammunition in the middle of the night. We always felt safe among the familiar dark silhouettes of the Carrier Battle Group, and when we came to leave to return to our solitary post, we had to steel ourselves to do so and hide our fear at what the next day's battle might bring. Sandy Woodward's well-meant words of encouragement – 'There is,' he said, 'only the second eleven left' – did not help much. One sailor, always ready to display his wit, made us all chuckle when commenting on the award of a medal for this conflict; he reckoned that those serving in the big ships of the Battle Group would qualify for the Burma Star because they were always so far to the east.

Whenever we had survived another long day and darkness finally came to give us some measure of protection, I used to sit down in my cabin with a glass of port, a King Edward cigar and a Mozart concerto. This was sheer heaven. I had always taken a radio-cassette player and a collection of tapes with me in ships, though now I only had a limited selection with me. Mozart had always been a favourite and I found the music calming and consoling, and I loved listening to the piano. If I had had some opera duets or a recording of choral music, I might just as easily have listened to those: I was always readily transported to another world when I heard a cathedral choir singing anthems or psalms.

A cigar and a glass of port were normally only things I indulged in after a formal dinner ashore. But on these occasions, it was an encouragement to sit down and enjoy a few precious moments of relaxation. The taste of the cigar was always sweet and the music exquisite and sublime – perfect, in fact. I have tried since to repeat the experience but that particular type of cigar has never tasted quite the same and nor have the piano concertos, especially the 21st and 23rd, ever sounded quite so magical. Perhaps it all has something to do with the flow of adrenalin in the human body: in war this is invariably increased and so all our senses become much more acute. But that music can still bring tears to my eyes, for it takes me straight back to those times.

Every day was critical as we listened to the air war raging above and around us. The Harriers were forever active, harrying and outmanoeuvring the enemy, scoring hits each time. Ships in the Sound, and later the Rapiers, were also accounting for a few kills. I had a first-class fighter controller in Sub-Lieutenant Andy Moll, who directed the Harriers very effectively: in one raid, there were four aircraft flying close together and they shot down three out of the four; the fourth fled. It was a battle of attrition, one which the Harriers, with the help of ship-borne weapons, appeared to be winning.

However, there were still losses to bear: *Antelope* was attacked on 23 May and hit by two bombs which failed to explode. One man was killed. Later, a bomb blew up and killed the Royal

Engineer sergeant who was attempting to defuse it and badly wounded the other member of the disposal team. Within seconds, the ship was ablaze. Commander Nick Tobin gave the order to abandon ship in good time. 'The ship's company were taken off by landing craft,' he later recalled. 'I think I was the last to leave her. I climbed down a knotted rope into a landing craft. I felt a sense of shock, probably more frustration than anything else. I felt cheated. It all happened so quickly. The men were all very calm indeed.' Then, as the fire reached the ship's magazines, a massive explosion illuminated the night sky and broke the ship in two, and she sank.

I began to realize just how vulnerable we were becoming as we remained exposed for long periods in waters very close to where the enemy was concentrating his air activity. Following the loss of *Antelope*, I wondered when my turn might come and what damage *Coventry* might sustain; it just seemed a matter of time. But I was still confident in our ability to survive and only ever thought in terms of damage rather than destruction. That said, at one time I did study the chart and look for a suitable place along the north shore of West Falkland to beach the ship should it be so badly damaged that it might sink. I marked the spot mentally and kept the plan to myself. I am not sure now whether this was such a good idea as the ship would have become, quite literally, a sitting target, but it shows how much one tried to consider every contingency. Beaching a ship was never something that was taught or practised in the Navy. Indeed, the emphasis in our training was on how to avoid the beach – unless, of course, you were in charge of landing craft. To this day, I cannot remember quite why I came up with the idea or what I thought would be achieved by it.

There were days when the weather was fine in our area but the Battle Group was swathed in fog, which meant that the Harriers could not fly; they could take off in such conditions but not land back on board safely. These were desperate hours when the ships in the Sound were being pounded from the air and there were no Harriers to take the heat off them: I came to dread the quiet and distinctive tones of the senior interpreter on board as he informed me of the next wave of bombers on their way. As it was, even when the Harriers could fly, their time with us was short; *Coventry*'s control was therefore crucial to get them positioned to intercept the enemy in the quickest possible time and this called for the greatest of skill.

All the while, my interpreters were listening to the enemy air commanders on the mainland and absorbing a wealth of information. We knew exactly when aircraft were taking off and what type they were, just as we knew their numbers and their targets. At times, though, it was clear the Argentinians were having problems finding enough aircraft to make a sortie viable. We could also tell from the pilots' conversations in the air that their morale was suffering as squadrons were merged with others to compensate for losses: once in the air, the pilots would radio back to base their names and next-of-kin addresses in case they did not return. All this information was relayed to me on an internal line on my headset, and the essentials were passed to the ships in the Sound. It was clearly an advantage to know as much as we did of the enemy's intentions, but I felt we almost knew too much. It made us all too anxious.

Whenever attacks were imminent, we took damage-control measures. Routinely, it took no more than four minutes to shut all watertight hatches and close up full first-aid, fire-fighting and damage-control parties in the bases forward and aft. In the light of what had happened to *Sheffield*, the normal practice of battening down all hatches at action stations was questioned. It was not easy for those below decks to be effectively sealed up in compartments when they would have preferred to have a hatch open to provide a quicker escape upwards. At the same time, we needed as much as possible to preserve the watertight integrity of the ship's hull in order to withstand damage and remain afloat. It was a difficult balance. In the end, I did allow some hatches to remain open, since this both allowed more ease of movement within the ship and allayed some people's anxieties. A further lesson we learned from other ships' experience was that our gas masks, which had been designed to protect against chemical attack or nuclear fallout, could nevertheless be used to prevent suffocation in thick smoke, even if only for a short time. We therefore made sure everyone kept their gas mask with them at all times.

Monday, 24 May, was another difficult day. We directed the Harriers and, as usual, they performed wonderfully. Several Skyhawks and Daggers were either shot down or damaged, some of the latter ditching in the sea as they tried to get home. The ships in the Sound survived by the narrowest of margins, although three of the large landing ships, RFA *Sir Galahad* and two of her sisters, were damaged. In one case, a 1,000-pound bomb failed to explode inside its target: the Argentinians were clearly still having trouble with the fuses of their bombs when these were launched at low level.

This, perhaps, requires further explanation. An Argentinian Skyhawk, for example, would carry its bombs on horizontal racks under the wings. When they were released at some 400 mph at low level and close to the target, these bombs were given a significant forward momentum as well as a destructive power capable of penetrating the hull of any ship. Towards the end of their unguided flight, however, they would inevitably begin to fall as they lost speed, so the pilot had to release them at exactly the right range to get them into a ship. Otherwise, they would under- or overshoot harmlessly. A correctly delayed fuse, always assuming it worked, would initiate an explosion when a bomb was fully embedded in a ship. But the fuses the Argentinians were using were primarily designed to be triggered when a bomb was dropped from a height and fell more or less vertically downwards over a longer period of time – hence the failure of many of their bombs to explode. Unsurprisingly, all of us fervently hoped this would remain the case. Yet, in one of its many announcements, the BBC had volunteered the information that the enemy's bombs had not been exploding on impact with our ships. This may well have been the first the Argentinians knew of the problem, and it probably galvanized them into modifying their fuses so that they set off an explosion after a shorter and more horizontal flight. Whatever the truth, *Coventry* was going to suffer for it.

The enemy's bombs, incidentally, were British-made. We had also, of course, sold the Argentinian Navy one Type 42 destroyer and provided plans for another to be built in South America. The enemy was therefore all too familiar with the limitations of the Sea Dart system and knew exactly how to conduct attacks against ships such as *Coventry*. Such are the ironies of the international arms trade.

As it was, *Coventry* had escaped attack on 24 May, although we now knew we had been spotted by the enemy and our position reported. There was an Argentinian observation post on Mount Rosalie, West Falkland, which looked out towards our area of operations, and ominously, we had seen some returning Skyhawks flying within sight of us, though out of our weapon range. I concluded that it made sense for us to move and asked the off-watch principal warfare officer, Clive Gwilliam, to draft a firm signal to Sandy Woodward saying that I considered we should not stay here any longer, giving reasons why. The signal remained on the bridge for me to look at when I had time and, had events not overtaken us, it would in due course have been sent.

We would all have felt safer had the weather behaved as it normally did at this time of year in the South Atlantic. Instead, it favoured the enemy: blue skies, good visibility and smooth seas provided ideal flying conditions. I would have been much happier with low cloud, poor visibility, strong winds and rough seas: we were entirely familiar with these conditions and fought well in them. But whatever the weather, I knew I could do my job. I was very conscious of being the product of the Royal Navy's unique traditions and training systems, and this gave me the confidence I needed, just as it steeled me to withstand the pressures. Furthermore, as the losses of men and ships accumulated all around me, I found myself becoming much more aggressive and angry towards the enemy – totally uncompromising, in fact. The cares or anxieties of peacetime had long since ceased to impinge on me. Earlier, for example, in the wake of some rough weather and violent manoeuvring, I had found all my brandy glasses in pieces on the deck of my cabin after they had been hurled out of a cupboard. I had just left them where they lay, thinking how totally immaterial or irrelevant it was to worry about such things at such a time. (It embarrasses me, even now, to think I still had these items on board in a war situation.) In a similar vein, I was proud of the weather-beaten, rust-streaked look of the ship and its peeling paint. We really did resemble a veteran man-of-war and I think we relished all the dangers and challenges.

Back in England, D was understandably anxious following the recent attacks on our ships. On 24 May she wrote: 'I seem to be so taken up with looking after *Coventry* families that I find I hardly have a moment to write to you. This weekend, as you can imagine, was a bad time. The minute the news broke that five ships had been hit and two of them badly, the telephone started ringing and went on until 3 a.m. Distraught mothers of sailors were asking if I had any news of *Coventry* – eventually I rang Northwood and said I must have something to tell families and they simply said, "There is no news that *Coventry* has been hit," so at least I could tell the mothers that. I also said no news is good news and they would really do best to go to bed and have a good sleep. I'm so tired in the evenings that I simply go straight to sleep, whatever the situation, and was rather put out to be woken up throughout the night. However, I think it reassures them to talk to a fairly calm voice – and if it helps them a bit, then it's worthwhile.

'We all feel stunned at the thought of those young lives being lost and ships that took years to design and build sinking in a matter of hours. And the helicopter losses are so tragic – particularly when it is an accident. Oh dear – how mad and wasteful it all seems, but when it's all over at least we will have taught the world a lesson: that aggression simply doesn't pay. But at what a cost of lives and ships. Not only do all the families feel very proud of you all in the Task Force, but the whole country is solidly behind you. And, as I tell some worried parents, I have the utmost faith in your professional ability to bring the ship safely home – at which they look most relieved. I know you don't like me saying such things, but I am a very proud wife, and I feel perfectly calm and strong because I have such faith in you.

'Last week I much enjoyed dinner at HMS *Nelson*. Everyone looked after me so beautifully – and I came away feeling most cherished and rather special. I really can't say enough about the support and kindness from the Navy, and from so many individuals and friends who put themselves out to ring at the worst moments. It is really very touching – and I know they are doing it for your sake as well as mine. One or two mothers and fathers of people in *Coventry* have written to say how happy their sons are in the ship and what a lot they think of you – which is so nice.

'Life is so busy there is never a dull moment – but all the time we just pray for peace and an end to the fighting. Apart from your wife and daughters who love you dearly, you have so many friends and relations who care very much about you and are much concerned for your welfare – so please do make sure you come back safely and unscathed. I don't allow myself to dwell on how much danger you are in; I simply live from day to day and think only of the marvellous day you get home. I doubt if I will let you out of my sight again after these few months.'

For my part, I do not think I ever doubted that I would get home, or that I would not be back for my August family holiday in Cornwall. That was my aiming point in the back of my mind and the most important thing to be looking forward to. In retrospect, though, I had no reason to be confident that I would return safely considering the number of people and ships that had already been lost and would never return home. But it is often just such a feeling of invulnerability that drives people on despite the odds against them; and the longer you survive, the stronger that feeling becomes. This seems to be part and parcel of human nature, yet it flies in the face of logic and reality.

We were all very aware that 25 May, Argentina's National Day, would stir the enemy into producing his best and most determined effort. None the less, I was convinced that if I could survive 25 May, I could survive the war. One way or another, the day had all the makings of a fight to the finish: it would be touch and go, both for *Coventry* and the outcome of the war.

In May 1941, another *Coventry*, the anti-aircraft cruiser, had been fighting off the Mediterranean island of Crete in support of the evacuation of the British, Commonwealth and Greek forces there. Many ships were being lost through relentless dive-bombing from the Luftwaffe but Admiral Cunningham, under great pressure to withdraw his fast-dwindling fleet to safety, had stood firm. Indeed, he had sent the following signal to his ships: 'It takes the Navy three years to build a ship. It would take three hundred years to build a new reputation. The evacuation will continue.' My own *Coventry* was deployed in the same anti-aircraft role as her predecessor. We may have been supporting British forces during a landing and consolidation ashore, but the circumstances were otherwise much the same. Admiral Cunningham's signal seemed just as apt in 1982 as it had been forty-one years earlier.

During the night of 24 May, I had a vivid dream of my twin brother Robert, who had been killed in a road accident when we were both twenty-five. I had never, as far as I could remember, dreamt about him before. He was sitting at a bare table in the middle of an empty room and crying. He seemed to be worrying about me. I was looking down on him from one end of the room and just said, 'Don't worry, I'll be all right.' As with most dreams, it faded quickly when I woke up and I thought no more about it. Besides, even if it had stayed with me, I doubt I would have spent long pondering what it meant. There simply wasn't the time.

CHAPTER 9

LAST STAND

From first light on 25 May, *Coventry* and *Broadsword* were braced for action, and when it came, it was fast and furious. Argentinian aircraft were detected heading for Falkland Sound to make their bombing runs on the ships there, but on this occasion they did not succeed in causing any damage. No doubt desperate to avoid the guns and missiles of the ships they had just attacked, they opened out to the north, towards us, before altering course to the west and home. As they gained height, we locked on to them with our radars and engaged with Sea Dart missiles. We destroyed one aircraft and then fired at another. At first, we thought we had missed the second one but the sight of a descending parachute confirmed a kill. About an hour later, another pair of aircraft turned towards us for an attack. We shot one down and the other fled towards the mainland.

The Harrier fighters which we helped to direct were on patrol during these raids but we held them off, assessing that our missiles offered the best and quickest option for attack. This was always a close call. Would the Harriers get there in time to intercept, especially if they were still on their way from the carriers? Or should we engage with missiles that were immediately to hand and the mere press of a button away from firing? The systems in *Coventry* which managed the initial detection of a target through to missile lock-on were of 1960s vintage, however, and so comparatively slow to reach the firing stage. Furthermore, a Harrier's Sidewinder missile would usually be more likely to achieve a kill than a Sea Dart. And there was always the deterrent effect of the Harriers: even if a target was out of range, the fact that they were in full cry towards the enemy was probably enough to scare them away and make them abort their attacks. In retrospect, this was a factor I probably underestimated.

During a short lull in air activity in the middle of the day, *Coventry* was surprised to receive a delivery of a package from a helicopter. How brave of the helicopter, I thought, to risk itself in this part of the world at this time of day. The package was for me: it was given to me on the bridge and contained a bottle of Pusser's Rum along with a letter from a lifelong friend wishing me good luck. While on a stay in the West Indies, this friend had given the bottle to the captain of the destroyer *Exeter*, Hugh Balfour, to give to me after he had completed his missile trials and come south to the Falklands. Hugh did as he had promised, sending the bottle over in his helicopter when his ship was in range of *Coventry* and regardless, it seemed, of anything else that might have been going on. This quite cheered me up. But it also occurred to me that perhaps Hugh thought we might not survive much longer, so he had better get his delivery over to me before it was too late. The bottle remained on the bridge in front of my chair throughout a very long day; there wasn't time to do anything else with it, and certainly not to drink it.

I am amused now to think of Hugh Balfour summoning his pilot to the bridge of *Exeter* for a briefing. The pilot must have been wondering what his mission would be and whether to load torpedoes or missiles: when he learnt what he was actually to do, he must have thought his captain had taken leave of his senses. But Hugh Balfour was a delightful individual, a man of ideas who was always keen to challenge any generally accepted naval wisdom. A free spirit, he was never going to be too inconvenienced by the enemy.

I quickly had to take my mind off the rum. Steering an easterly course at twelve knots, we received warning of a further raid on its way and gained radar contact at about 180 miles. As always, when the attackers made their landfall on the Falklands, they flew low over the hills and we lost contact. We knew they were close and *Broadsword*, which still had them on radar, was frantically giving me their position. But try as we might, we could not see them. Then suddenly we sighted them, both visually by the lookouts on the upper deck and on the radar, when they came clear of Pebble Island about ten miles to the south. Two aircraft, probably Skyhawks, were flying very fast and low straight towards us – below the level of the bridge – but it was too late to get my missiles anywhere near to firing. We engaged with the ship's main 4.5-inch gun, the 20-mm Oerlikons and machine guns. One aircraft was hit in the tail before our barrage of fire frightened them off. They then veered towards *Broadsword* astern of us and launched two bombs at her. One missed and passed overhead, while the other hit the sea, bounced, went through the quarterdeck, up through the flight deck and destroyed the helicopter. It did not explode, however, and landed in the sea clear of the ship, causing no further damage.

We had been lucky so far, although it was extremely unfortunate that *Broadsword* had not been able to engage the aircraft with her Sea Wolf missiles. We learnt later that she had had the pair of Skyhawks clearly in her missile sights but the system would not lock on to either of them and actually switched off at the critical moment. The system's software had a limitation: it could not decide which target to fire at when two aircraft were flying close together and at the same range. So an opportunity was lost and the enemy aircraft got away. Perhaps if *Broadsword* had shot down even one of them, they might have thought twice about trying again.

However, this was probably wishful thinking as the Argentinians were clearly determined to take out *Coventry*. After all, we were being a considerable nuisance and they no doubt knew that we were directing the Harriers and coordinating the defence of the Landing Force and the ships in the Sound. Whether they had also discovered that we were eavesdropping on their conversations, we never found out.

Everything was happening very quickly now. Less than a minute after this attack, another was developing. But where were they? We didn't know. We thought there might be four of them, Skyhawks and possibly Mirages, split into pairs and coming from two different directions. There was no information from *Broadsword*. Lieutenant David Walton, the principal warfare officer, said: 'It's the ones to the north-west that we want to worry about.' That didn't make sense. I looked hard but couldn't see them on my radar set. I turned to Lieutenant-

Commander Dick Lane, the air warfare officer on my left, who was searching for targets and preparing Sea Dart for action. There was nothing definite on his plot and no missile lock-on. A second later, aircraft were detected to the south, and I ordered the ship to alter course to starboard to ensure Sea Dart had a clear view of them. Two Harriers were on the way and they had sight of the enemy.

Dick Lane reported a lock-on. The fighter controller, Sub-Lieutenant Andy Moll, stood up in front of me and shouted: 'Do you want a Harrier to come in?' It didn't look as though it could quite get there in time and Sea Dart was ready to go. I said: 'Hold it off.' We fired a Sea Dart, but it didn't hit anything and slammed into the hills. Suddenly, two aircraft were sighted from the bridge coming straight for us, about 20 degrees on the port bow, very fast and so low that water sprayed up behind them. We opened fire with the 4.5-inch, the Oerlikons and all the small arms we could muster. In desperation, Petty Officer David Nuttall, the yeoman of signals, ordered Radio Operator Trev Trevarthen to try and blind the pilots' eyes by switching on the powerful signalling projector and pointing it directly at them. Then the port Oerlikon jammed. Leading Seaman Brian Smith, on the gun direction platform nearby, leapt to the gun to get it firing again.

A dreadful silence ensued. We felt utterly helpless. The entire operations room team of some thirty-five people had been frantically trying to detect these targets and to bring all our weapons to bear on them, but now there was simply nothing else to be done. And it seemed a particularly long, agonizing and ominous silence, even though it must only have lasted for a few seconds.

Both aircraft got through and released their bombs. One also strafed the ship's side and the hangar area with cannon fire. One bomb missed and flew overhead, but three bombs tore into the port side of the ship and ripped their destructive paths downwards through steel decks before coming to rest deep down inside the hull.

Broadsword, still recovering from the earlier attack and trying to cope with this one, found *Coventry* blocking her view of the targets heading straight for us and so she was unable to fire her Sea Wolf for fear of hitting us in the process. In these frantic split seconds *Broadsword* had no time to react and manoeuvre into a better firing position, and this left the enemy free to press home his attack. Our plan of remaining at slow speed so that *Broadsword* would be able to accelerate clear of *Coventry* and confront an incoming raid head-on had not worked. We had been outwitted by the enemy, whose carefully planned attack, along with a certain amount of luck on his part, had won him the day. The aircraft's approach on the bow rather than on the beam had probably increased the chances of the bombs hitting the ship and embedding themselves in it, rather than passing over the top or straight through, as had happened with *Glasgow*. By springing out from over the land such a short distance away, the Argentinian pilots had simply been too cunning for us and too quick.

The sinister silence in *Coventry* was abruptly shattered by two 1,000-pound bombs exploding. In the operations room there was a vicious shockwave, a blinding flash and searing heat. I felt as though I had been caught in a doorway and a heavy door had been slammed against me: the force and the shock of the impact shook my whole body to the core. I was stunned into unconsciousness. When I came to my senses, I was still sitting, very precariously, on the edge of my now broken chair in front of the radar screen into which I had been peering intently a few seconds before. But the screen was no longer there: it had simply disintegrated. I had been gripping the handle fitted to the front of the screen as I leant forward to take a closer look and tried to steady myself while the ship manoeuvred and tossed in the sea. This, I think, must have saved me from being thrown across the room by the blast, just as the radar screen must have momentarily shielded me from the worst of the shockwaves before it shattered into pieces.

My headset and microphone had disappeared – burnt off me without a trace. So too had my anti-flash hood and gloves save for a few shreds around my wrists. I was neither aware of any injuries nor concerned about them. I looked to my left and saw a sheet of orange flame leap out of the hatch down into the computer room below and envelop a man as he attempted to climb up into the operations room. He had nearly reached the top of the ladder, and someone had stretched towards him and tried to catch his hand. But it was too late: consumed by fire, he could go no further and fell back with a final, despairing cry for help. In the hellish furnace that the computer room had become were seven key members of the weapons engineering department, among them Lieutenant Rod Heath, their leader. The blast of the bomb would have killed the majority of them outright.

Most of the operations room team seemed to have disappeared: they had been blown off their feet and pushed across into corners of the room where they lay awkwardly among pieces of wrecked equipment, stunned and apparently lifeless. Commander Geoff Lane was no longer in his position by the general operations plot behind me: he now found himself on the deck on the far side with burns on his face, hands and head where his headset had melted into his scalp. He had had to beat out the flames on his own head. Dick Lane, who had been managing the air picture and Sea Dart, was nowhere to be seen, nor was David Walton, who had been looking after the surface and action plot and should have been just to my right. Seconds before, these two officers had been my trusted advisers and fully engaged in trying to defend the ship from the aircraft screaming towards us at wave-top height. Both suffered burns to their hands and faces but Dick Lane came off worse as he was closer to the computer-room hatch through which the bomb had blasted its heat and flame: his legs were burnt as well.

I looked all about me in the darkness. There was nothing to be seen in the thick black smoke except a few dim shapes of people, behind me and to my left, struggling and with their clothes alight: I could hear their plaintive cries. Nothing and no one was recognizable, but I knew that among these dim shapes were Chief Petty Officers 'Eli' Ellis and Philip Fisher, respectively the Sea Dart controller and 4.5-inch gun director, and Petty Officer Chris Howe, the electronic warfare specialist, all of whom suffered terribly in the blast. Much of their clothing was burnt off and their flesh exposed to the intense heat. Lieutenant-Commander Ian Young, the deputy weapons engineer officer, had been standing behind the Sea Dart operators, also to my left, ready to spot the slightest faltering in the technology that might prejudice a successful firing. He was blasted off his feet and set alight like a human torch: he was there one second and gone the next. I was not to see him or the others again for several weeks.

There were small fires flickering and leaping around on the

deck like giant candles, probably the result of signal pads catching fire. The many chairs positioned around the various consoles and screens and firmly bolted to the deck had gone: they were reduced to twisted tubes of steel which lay all around and caused people to stumble and trip as they began to scramble to their feet, choking in the smoke and looking for a way out. I heard voices encouraging and calming people as they coaxed them to an exit and towards safer areas of the ship. After a time, I found I was alone. I had probably been knocked senseless for longer than most, but now I too quickly began to look for an escape.

As far as it was possible to tell in this blackest of glooms, the ladder behind me which led to the bridge via the cabin flat was severely twisted and broken. So I went over to the door on the left-hand (port) side which led into the main passage and in so doing stumbled over broken bits and pieces strewn on the deck, bruising my shins. As I got near to the door, all I could see was a wall of fire and terrible destruction. The smoke was getting thicker and more acrid all the time and I was no nearer to finding a way out. I returned to the centre of the operations room and considered my situation. I could see no way out and I was suffocating. For some reason, I did not attempt to go out of the starboard side door into the passageway: besides, I could not see it and at the time I sensed it was impassable. There was no alternative but to die and so I prepared myself accordingly. Suffocation begins with a welcome calming effect, yet it is only one small step away from collapse and death. I was not far from it.

Dick Lane later described his experience: 'I had been caught in a fireball, knocked out of my chair, hurled across the operations room and came to, several seconds later, underneath a radar display that had fallen over me. The sights and sounds were horrific. Pockets of little fires spread over the deck, cabling was sparking, people moving slowly, emergency lights only, smoke, the screams of someone down in the computer room below. I crawled over to try and pull him out but he slipped from my grasp and fell back into the inferno that had been his work station a few seconds before.

'As I got to my feet, it became clear to me very quickly that the ship was in terminal decline. It was heeling at a ridiculous angle and it was getting worse. The first bomb had entered the ship just forward of the computer-room below us in the operations room. The subsequent explosion created a fireball that came out of the computer-room hatch and flew through the operations room, creating devastation in its wake. One minute I was defending the ship against attack and now I was dazed and hurting in the corner of the operations room.'

The first bomb went into the ship's port side below the bridge, three or four feet above the waterline, leaving a hole about two feet across; it crashed and spiralled its way down, first through 2 deck passageway, then 3 deck by the computer room and finally down into the conversion machinery room on 4 deck, where it exploded. It blew a huge hole in the side below the waterline and in the transverse bulkhead leading to the adjacent storeroom compartment. Instantly, the water rushed in, first to the machinery room and then into the storerooms, creating a huge water-filled area in the heart of the ship, and as *Coventry* listed to port, the water rose rapidly to 3 deck, and then to 2 deck, where the original entry hole became submerged, allowing even more water in. The upward blast, together with fire and smoke, went directly into the computer room and upwards again into the operations room, pushing the whole deck about two feet upwards.

Able Seaman Mick Daniels, who had been working the sonar in the operations room, later recalled: 'I crept over to the electronic plot to watch the raid coming in as two HA (hostile aircraft) markings got closer and closer. We seemed to throw everything at them, then I sensed a quietness of anticipation. I crouched down as I heard a couple of loud whooshes. As I stood up, thinking the danger had passed, there were the most beautiful colours of orange and red – I had never seen the operations room lit before – everything was silhouetted, I could see shapes of people and equipment, it was then like slow motion, I was travelling backwards trying to grab anything to stop me, but not succeeding and I ended up in the far corner of the room by the underwater telephone position. When I got to my feet, there was a deathly silence and lots of things were glowing brightly, then there were things floating down from above, like hundreds of feathers after a pillow fight. I was covered in them. It was so strange for a place which was always so clean and sterile. My respirator, lifejacket and survival suit, along with my diary, all disappeared for good.'

The ship might have been able to survive this bomb explosion if the damage-control teams had managed to create a watertight boundary to contain the flooding and fire. *Coventry* was divided into many sections divided by transverse bulkheads running from one side of the ship to the other between each deck level, which allowed a number of them to be flooded before the ship was in danger of sinking. But, as luck would have it, split seconds after the first bomb had hit, a second went into the ship's superstructure above the engine room; it punched gaping holes in the decks as it hurtled down past the forward auxiliary machinery room and through to the forward engine room on 4 deck, and then exploded. A large hole, some ten feet long and three feet wide, was blown in the ship's side on the waterline; critically, the transverse bulkhead that separated the forward and the after engine rooms was also holed by the blast. Watch-keepers had time to observe the hole in the side and began to make a report to the machinery control room when the explosion occurred. As the ship began to heel over, the waters of the South Atlantic thundered into both engine rooms, reaching up to 2 deck level. It was all too much for *Coventry* to bear.

The blast, fire and smoke from this bomb rocketed instantly upwards to the junior ratings' dining room, machinery control room, main damage-control headquarters and the technical office, all on 2 deck. The dining room was virtually destroyed. Five ratings who made up a damage-control and first-aid team based in the dining room, four engineer ratings in the forward engine room and one in the technical office were all killed by the blast. Petty Officer Michael 'Foxy' Fowler, the leader of the sonar team and damage-control expert, was among those killed in the dining room.

A third bomb penetrated the superstructure in the port waist and spun downwards through 2 deck and 3 deck, leaving large holes in both, before landing in the storerooms on 4 deck, not far from the first bomb – but it did not explode. However, the holes in the decks allowed smoke and fire to spread uncontrollably. Two communications ratings found themselves trapped in a transmitter equipment office on 2 deck when the door was blown off and a large hole appeared in the deck outside in the passageway through which flames were flaring. They were in shock and unable to move. It would take a very brave man to rescue them.

The sheer weight of water and the devastating bomb damage on the port side of the ship, forward and amidships, caused it to list rapidly to an acute angle. The situation could not have been worse with both engine rooms, the largest compartments in the ship, opened up to the sea. As the angle increased, the damage and penetrations in the side from one of the Skyhawks' cannon fire caused even more flooding. Some watertight doors in the port passageway running the length of the ship had been blown off or damaged, and this allowed both the water and lethal smoke to penetrate further. Damage-control parties faced a formidable task under appalling conditions, with shock, fire, smoke and the sea pouring into the ship. Seventeen men had been killed and at least twice as many injured – seven in the operations room alone were badly burnt and ended up being taken to SS *Uganda*, the hospital ship, for treatment. Amazingly, no one in the operations room was killed but all were too shocked or injured to play any part in trying to fight the fires or save the ship.

Lieutenant-Commander Rob Hamilton, who had been in the damage-control headquarters towards the rear of the ship, later described the moments after the explosions: 'When we heard the Oerlikons firing, we knew we were into a close-quarters fight. Then came the order, "Brace, brace, brace!" I remember a loud bang as if someone had slammed a heavy door. Almost simultaneously, someone in the machinery control centre shouted that we had lost a fire pump, giving a clue as to what the bomb had hit. Ten seconds after the first bang, there was a most terrific crash as the bomb detonated some fifteen feet from where I was sitting on the deck in the HQ. My face, which was between my knees, felt as if someone had pushed a million pins and needles into it. When I recovered my senses and looked around me, the machinery control room and adjacent technical office were in a state of total disarray. The entire area was smoke-logged down to two or three feet above the deck. It seemed there was little any of us could do so I ordered that we should immediately evacuate the headquarters.'

With the damage-control headquarters out of action, it was impossible to coordinate any damage limitation by establishing fire, smoke and flood boundaries in the way that we had rehearsed so often. On trying to leave the headquarters by the port exit, one rating looking forward along the passage could see the sea through the deck. Only the starboard exit could be used. The after damage-control base became the temporary command centre, but it soon had to be abandoned as well. All machinery and the ship's engines had stopped and there was no means of communication between damage-control, fire-fighting and first-aid teams. With the steeply sloping decks and broken ladders, let alone with the fire and the smoke, it was difficult to move about and do anything to save the ship. We now depended on the initiative and bravery of individuals to rescue people and get them to safety. Rob Hamilton knew the ship was in danger of capsizing and so he calmly ordered his men to get to the upper deck before more lives were lost. He had tried beforehand to telephone the bridge to inform the officer-of-the-watch of the situation below decks, but the telephone was not working. Nothing, in fact, was working.

Several people, instead of getting themselves to the upper deck and comparative safety, went in search of others whom they suspected had been trapped, shocked or disorientated and needed assistance in finding their way out. The risks were very great as the ship heeled over and the smoke thickened; some put on their gas masks to give themselves more time to search for others before they in turn were overcome. Chief Petty Officer Tyrone Smith was just one of several senior engineer ratings who calmly ensured an orderly evacuation of smoke-filled compartments. Then, as the ship began to be abandoned and after he had escorted a number of ratings to safety on the upper deck, he returned below decks again to attempt fire-fighting. But even though Smith, too, was eventually beaten back by the rapid, uncontrollable flooding and the smoke, he still had the presence of mind to brief ratings to keep clear of the ship's propellers when jumping into the sea and thus undoubtedly saved their lives.

Towards the bows of the ship on 2 deck, Chief Petty Officer Tom Sutton's forward damage-control party heard the two huge bomb explosions followed by a sickening vibration rattling through the ship's structure, whereupon almost immediately the ship began to lean to port. Sutton kept control of his men to ensure the forward section of the ship was cleared of personnel when it became necessary to abandon the area. He was instrumental in guiding to safety many shocked and injured men from the smoke-filled operations room, saving many lives. By this time, the ship was listing heavily and many ladders and exit routes were impassable. When he eventually came to save himself and jump overboard, Sutton immediately went to the aid of a badly burnt rating struggling in the water without a lifejacket and dragged him to a life-raft, thereby saving this man's life.

Indeed, the absolute priority for the remainder of this traumatic day was to save lives, for there was nothing we could do now for *Coventry*, with so much of her side opened up to the sea. Many men were rescued, and often in the most difficult of situations. Ladders to the upper deck – mostly twisted, some swinging freely, and all now at impossible angles as the ship leaned over – were only one of the hazards facing those trying to get the injured and concussed up and out of danger. But the ladders were nothing compared to the smoke, the heat and the fire. It was going to take acts of astonishing courage for some to be saved. And miracles too.

CHAPTER 10

RESCUE

I had been trapped in the dark and devastated operations room of *Coventry*, semi-conscious and suffocating. I had heard a few urgent voices of authority summoning help and maintaining order. But I had run out of options. I had thought of home and, ridiculous as it seems now, wondered who was going to mow the lawn in my absence. Then my mind had gone blank.

Suddenly, and I really don't know how much later this was, I found myself in clearer air in the starboard passageway not far from the operations room. I have no recollection at all of how I got there, but I suddenly became fully alert, or so I thought, and was intent on getting to the bridge as fast as possible. I made my way aft and eventually up twisted ladders through heat and thickening smoke along a back route towards the bridge from where I thought I could exercise some authority and get the ship heading in the right direction.

I turned to go into the officers' cabin area which would have taken me past the main entrance to my cabin and along the passage to the familiar ladder to the bridge, but there was no way through on account of the smoke and heat. I turned back and eventually tried another way and found a ladder still intact which took me up to the flag deck at the back of the bridge. I then continued forward, intent on entering the port door into the bridge, but I found it deserted and filled with smoke and fire billowing up through an open hatch. It was untenable and anyway I could not get in. I stayed on the port bridge wing, paused for breath and tried to take in what was happening. I fell to my knees to help my breathing and coughed and spluttered for a short time. I then saw Lieutenant-Commander Mike O'Connell and ordered him to get the ship going fast to the east. I had reckoned that this would get us into safer waters and nearer to help. He calmly replied, 'Aye, aye sir,' in the traditional manner and went away as if to do it.

I had no idea at that moment how absurd my order was. It was clear that *Coventry* was not going to go anywhere, as I am sure Mike O'Connell must have known. All power and communication were lost, the ship was stopped, burning furiously and beginning to roll over. I felt *Coventry* make a sudden movement as it listed about twenty degrees to port. It was an alarming sensation and I somehow knew these were the ship's death throes. One is so used to the movement of a ship at sea as it partly resists and partly moves with the force of the water, often in harmony with it, that when you feel a totally strange and awkward movement, you know at once that something is dreadfully wrong. It is rather like, I imagine, when the once firm ground around you starts shaking and giving way under your feet in an earthquake. You feel helpless, afraid and unable to do anything about it – and your whole, familiar world seems about to end. It felt like that now.

At this point, I became aware that my wrists and, to a lesser extent, my hands, had been burnt, and my face felt hot from the flash of the bomb explosion, as though I had been exposed to the hot sun for too long. My anti-flash gloves and hood had absorbed most of the heat before being shredded and blown off. As I had already noticed, some parts of the gloves which contained some elastic material to bind them tightly around the wrist remained on me: this is where the burns were worst and pieces of skin were hanging loose. It was the rubber content of the elastic that must have melted into my skin. I removed the skin and the remains of the gloves. Otherwise I felt unharmed, though I had clearly inhaled a considerable amount of smoke.

The deck was now at an alarming angle and between decks the ship was rapidly becoming a furnace from end to end. I climbed the now steep slope to the starboard side and witnessed the ship's company abandoning ship. It was all remarkably orderly and calm, looking just like a peacetime exercise. Hardly a word seemed to be spoken: it just happened. I never discovered who gave the general order to abandon ship. Perhaps no one did. But people very sensibly just carried on and did it. It was the only thing to do. I presume I had been considered a casualty and no longer fit to command the ship or give any orders. This was entirely understandable, for I had been one of the last ones to get up to the upper deck.

All the starboard-side life-rafts were now in the water and people were jumping into the sea to get into them. I looked on both intently and calmly, almost as though I was watching a film, and then moved down to the forecastle to prepare to leave the ship. People were helping each other to put on their lifejackets and 'once only' survival suits. These suits were essential if you were to survive for any length of time in the cold waters of the South Atlantic. It is hard enough to get into them under normal circumstances – they are like a modern-day surfer's wetsuit – and I was fortunate in that someone helped me with mine as my hands were painful and making things difficult. I don't remember who the sailor was and I would still like to thank him if ever I discover who he was. After all, he must have been pretty keen to save himself.

Able Seaman Izzy Isaacs later recalled his last minutes on the ship: 'The flight team was trying to get the helicopter airborne but the ship was listing too much and it had to be shut down. The senior rating of the flight then told us to sit on the hangar floor and put on our lifejackets. In the meantime, the helicopter had been lashed down so we moved out on to the flight deck by climbing up the starboard side. By this time water was beginning to come over the port side of the flight deck so we pulled the nets up to help us get over the side more easily if the order came to abandon ship. Somebody had released the life-rafts from the starboard side of the hangar – I realized then I had time to put on my survival suit and did so by hanging on to the nets with one hand and pulling it on with the other. My camera slipped out of my gas mask case and slid down across the flight deck, under the helicopter and over the side. I remember being very annoyed at my camera getting wet. People began climbing over the side – it was time to forget the camera. I looked over the side and was shocked to see one of the propellers exactly where I would have jumped, so I shouted a warning and moved forward, climbed on to the ship's side and slid into the water – boy, it was cold! I then swam to a life-raft.'

The ship was now almost on her beam ends. Some had to be

forcefully persuaded to jump over the side. This was particularly true of one of the Chinese laundrymen who could not swim. I was being implored to leave by people shouting to me from their life-rafts. The time had clearly come. When I had seen everyone jump into the sea and get into life-rafts, I walked down the ship's side, jumped the last two feet into the water and swam to a life-raft about twenty yards away. I was not aware of being cold in the water and took my time. When I got to the life-raft, I was pulled into it by someone with a cheerful smile who said, 'There you are, sir, it worked.' It was the petty officer who had given me the prayer, which was still in my pocket.

The life-raft I was in, with some thirty-five other survivors, drifted from the starboard side of the ship, around the bows, then got sucked into the hull, ending close up against the over-hanging port bow. We were in danger of being taken down by the ship as it rolled over on top of us. But then the life-raft was punctured by the sharp antenna on the nose of the one Sea Dart missile still on the launcher and most of us ended up in the water again. (I was reminded later by someone that I had suffered the ignominy of being sunk twice in one day.) By this time, however, the sky was full of helicopters and a boat from *Broadsword* was also in sight to pull people out of the water. One helicopter hovered over our deflated life-raft and hauled most of us to safety, and we were duly taken, along with others, to *Broadsword*. Another actually touched down on *Coventry*'s side, by this time burning red-hot within, to take off sailors who had scrambled on to it from the water. The pilots and crews of these helicopters displayed extraordinary skill and total commit-ment to saving our lives, quite regardless of the dangers to their own.

Chief Petty Officer Alf Tupper, a crewman of one of the helicopters sent out from San Carlos, viewed the scene from the air: 'Coventry had her hull upturned and was on fire. I was horrified. I had been in the Navy eighteen years and had never seen anything like that before. We could see quite a lot of life-rafts; they all looked very full and everyone was very wet and cold. One or two were badly shocked and I think some were burned.' Tupper was lowered down to sit on top of the life-rafts in order to help people, two or three at a time, into the harness on the end of the line from the helicopter that winched them up to safety. He was soaking wet himself but cleared three life-rafts of survivors in this way – more than sixty of them. The award he later received for his efforts was richly deserved.

While in the life-raft, I remember seeing one of the officers-under-training paddling alone in another small life-raft, commandeered from the helicopter flight, close along the submerged port side of the ship. He was a resourceful character and I thought it was typical of him to have abandoned the ship in his own personal life-raft. But he was in considerable danger of the ship rolling on top of him. I learnt that he had decided to take to the water over the port side as he had witnessed others sliding down the starboard side and injuring themselves on the keel of the ship. However, he soon got sucked in and trapped by the side of the ship near the Sea Dart launcher, whereupon his raft was also ruptured by the nose of the one remaining missile and began to sink. He was then forced to swim away to another life-raft, from where he was later rescued by helicopter. This officer went on to specialize in submarines: he preferred, he told me, to serve in vessels that were designed to sink beneath the waves.

Sub-Lieutenant Andy Moll vividly described his moment of leaving the ship: 'It is now ten minutes since the bombs came in. The ship is turning over fairly quickly and now has a 30–35 degree list. Lifejackets are now being passed around to those without, and as I have a "once only" suit, I decide to put it on. The angle of the deck is now too steep to accomplish this standing up so I sit down. As soon as my suit is half on, I toboggan through the cross passage to the portside. Bless the maker of guardrails which stop me going straight over the side, and I finish putting on the suit and lifejacket before moving. Decide not to jump off the port side with the ship heeling over on top of me, so struggle back up to the other side. Half a dozen people are with me, all debating whether to jump or slide down the ship's side. The stabilizers and bilge keel are now at water level so I decide to jump clear of them. Prepare to jump as someone grabs my arm. No idea who it is but he shouts, "Come on, sir," and together we jumped into the water.'

One of the remarkable things to witness was the way people took charge firmly and quietly and helped each other as much as they could. There was no evidence at all of the situation developing into panic, and no one seemed to be putting his own safety before that of others. Even more remarkable was the fact that, as a number of officers and senior ratings, especially in the operations room area, had effectively been taken out of action by the blast of the bombs, the whole process of preparing to abandon ship and then doing so had to be accomplished by more junior personnel. They were not the usual decision-makers in these situations, but they used their initiative and just got on with it, improvising as they went. It was these men who got as many life-rafts in the water as possible before the ship rolled over, and they had to move very fast to do so. They did an outstanding job in the midst of absolute turmoil.

None of the life-rafts on the port side of the ship could be released owing to the steep angle of the deck, so it was crucial that all those on the starboard side got into the water if there was going to be enough room in them for all the survivors. There were, in the end, just enough of them for everyone to find a space on board, although they had to accommodate twice the number of people for which they were designed. Most had anything up to forty survivors on board, which made them very crowded. Fortunately, the length of time spent in them was short, so the cramped conditions caused little harm.

Sub-Lieutenant Lee Jones, the resourceful young officer I had seen in his own life-raft, had only very recently joined the ship after graduating from the Naval Engineering College. Later, he committed his own memories of the sinking to paper: 'The incoming aircraft had caught the ship as she was weaving at speed and one of the bombs unluckily hit the engine room area, close to the waterline as the ship heeled to starboard. The second bomb penetrated the hull at 2 deck level below the bridge just where the computer room was located. Seconds after the impact, there were two almighty explosions close together and the ship started to list immediately. In a matter of minutes we had been rendered helpless, defenceless and without motive power. I was in a forward mess deck with Petty Officer Fallon, there was an eerie silence and increasing smoke was building up in the compartment. I made the decision that Fallon and I should both leave via the escape hatch above us and we both climbed the ladder up to it and squeezed through into another mess deck which led through to the ship's main passageway. I could see the vague outlines of personnel in the smoke moving forward. A voice was shouting, "Come along, move forward to the fo'c'sle escape hatch." I joined the mass of stumbling bodies.

'The smoke was bad and catching in my throat. As the orderly file of people reached the forward cross-passage, the line split and there was a senior rating at each ladder directing people upwards to the fo'c'sle. I remember thinking how businesslike the process was and had by this stage assumed the captain had given the order to abandon ship. In the meantime, the ship's list had increased to about 15 degrees. I was now on the fo'c'sle just aft of the breakwater screen and I helped people to put on their lifejackets and inflate them and generally make sure there was continued order amongst the twenty to thirty people gathered there.

'By this stage, the list was beginning to increase rapidly and I was concerned that the ship might capsize completely. Seeing the life-rafts in the water nearby, the crew started to jump into the water. The flow of jumpers increased – like lemmings off a cliff, I thought. As the list increased further, it became less of a jump, more a slide down the side of the hull.'

Most of the ship's company ended up in *Broadsword* – about 280 of us. She had just had a bomb through her flight deck, she was fighting a fire and there was still the threat of further air attacks, although the light was slowly fading. Despite all this, the ship processed this large number of bedraggled and shocked sailors through her rescue organization – stripping us, bathing us, reclothing us, keeping us warm and administering first aid. About twenty people were quite badly burnt and a larger number suffered, like me, from superficial flash burns. The more badly injured were flown straight to the hospital ship *Uganda* or to the Commando Brigade field dressing station at Ajax Bay in San Carlos. Commander Geoff Lane and Lieutenant-Commander Ian Young were taken first to Ajax Bay for treatment to their burns and then to the hospital ship. From there, with others, they were eventually taken to Montevideo by sea and then flown to the UK. Chris Howe was to remain in *Uganda* for about six weeks of treatment before he was fit enough to travel home.

It was a remarkable rescue operation and one which was conducted as though it had been practised for years. We were fortunate that there were no more air attacks that evening, although there was a protective umbrella of Harriers overhead as *Broadsword* and the helicopters worked furiously to get everyone on board before nightfall and, more importantly, before men succumbed and died in the icy water. We were also fortunate that the sea was quite calm.

Between them, Lieutenant Richard Bell-Davies and Sub-Lieutenant Clive Pickering in *Broadsword* took a series of photographs of *Coventry* from the moment the bombs exploded inside the ship until she was upside down with just the keel and propellers visible. The Navy now has these striking pictures in its archives and they appear frequently in the many books and articles written about the campaign. (You can, in fact, see them in the middle plate section here.) I have often wondered whether these officers were specifically instructed to be there with a camera in case there were any actions worth capturing on film, or whether they were off-watch when we were attacked and just happened to have a camera with them. Either way, they certainly took some astonishing photographs.

Air Engineer Mick Dilucia also had a camera with him but,

unable to get to the opening in his life-raft as so many were packed inside, he had to hand it to Chief Petty Officer Mick Pattison, who went on to take some good pictures of the ship on her side and of the rescue operation taking place. To take your camera with you when abandoning ship, and to manage somehow to prevent it from getting too wet, shows great presence of mind. The film was later developed in *QE2* and the prints provide a sobering record of this melancholy moment.

Stories of the British sailor's humour in adversity are legion, and there was no shortage of it, even on this terrifying day. In the heat of the action, a sailor on lookout duty on the starboard bridge wing was heard to shout, 'Mirage!' as he pointed frantically at an attacking aircraft. Without a pause, a quiet voice was heard to respond from inside the bridge, 'Looks fucking real to me, mate.' Later, in a life-raft and in clear sight of the sinking ship, a rating turned to an officer and asked, 'Are rounds tonight cancelled, sir?' ('Rounds' being the routine nightly inspection of mess decks for cleanliness and secure stowage.) Another young sailor, glancing out of his life-raft and seeing the mass of rescue helicopters, commented: 'All those helicopters – looks just like a bloody Fleet Air Arm air display.' Meanwhile, Radio Supervisor Sam MacFarlane remembers swimming towards a life-raft with a friendly face peering out who shouted, 'Give us your hand, mate, and climb in – standing room only but the beer's good.' So in he got.

Able Seaman Paul Inman would recall his own time in a life-raft: 'Once in the raft, there was silence. I do not remember any conversation. My thoughts turned towards home and what my Mum was going to think about all this when she heard about *Coventry*. It is strange that in certain circumstances we do certain things. I was sitting in a life-raft in the South Atlantic, my ship had just been lost and I started to recite a song called "Rat Trap" by the Boomtown Rats. Why this particular song, I do not know, it had no special meaning for me, yet here I was reciting it silently in my mind. To this day, whenever I hear this particular song I think of that life-raft.'

Traumatic events often become indelibly associated with the unlikely, even bizarre, images or sounds that enter into people's heads at the time. Paul Inman sought comfort from music, just as I had done earlier at the end of difficult days. He also had one other, very specific memory: 'I cannot remember what time I spent in the life-raft. I do, however, recall one of my shipmates shouting, "There she goes," indicating *Coventry* rolling over. I looked at my watch at that moment and it had stopped at 6.15, which must have been the time I jumped into the sea. I have that watch to this very day, the hands still showing 6.15.'

In extreme circumstances, you tend to lose any real sense of time passing. Every second can seem an eternity, and I have little doubt that the majority of *Coventry*'s company, struggling as they were to find a way out of the ship and to survive, were viewing everything in a sort of slow motion. Myself, I remember looking at the clock in the operations room before the attack began and registering that it was almost 6.15. Assuming Paul Inman's watch was telling the right time and did indeed stop when he entered the water, everything must therefore have happened very quickly. It is surprising, too, that some people were in the water within minutes of our being hit. Perhaps the bomb explosions and resulting damage were simply so catastrophic that the ship went over almost at once. It is unlikely we shall ever know the exact timing of events on this day.

Once on board *Broadsword*, I went to the bridge to see Bill Canning, just to show my face and let him know that I was alive. I thought that this fact might then be communicated to Sandy Woodward and thence home. He was, of course, very occupied, but he turned to me and said with great feeling, 'I'm very sorry, David.' It was all he could say. I was quite unable to say anything in return, such was the emotion of the moment. Bill Canning later recalled: 'What do you say to *Coventry*'s captain when he is ushered to your bridge sopping wet, frozen stiff and injured? "Would you like a warm bath?" seemed desperately inadequate.' I duly left the bridge and was taken to his cabin for that bath and a change of clothing.

Petty Officer Mick Stuart appeared from somewhere to help me as my hands were by now covered in ointment and encased in bandages. It was both a wonderful and extremely thoughtful gesture. It was while I was in the bath that I first became aware of how cold I was and I noticed that my legs were a deep shade of blue. After getting dressed and having a hot drink, I sat in the cabin awaiting developments. I was now a mere passenger, just waiting to be told what to do. I began to wonder who had survived the attack, for I had no idea yet as to the number of casualties. I did see Rob Hamilton, though, and I expressed my delight that he had been rescued and was in good shape.

The senior weapons engineer officer of *Broadsword*, Commander John Castle, came into the cabin and asked me, rather nervously, whether I would like to see my ship. He removed the darken-ship screen from the scuttle and I looked out to see *Coventry* for the last time; she was upside down a short distance away, with her keel showing just a few feet above the sea and her propellers projecting up in the air. Helicopters were still surrounding her as they carried out a final search for any survivors. Less than an hour earlier, my ship had been an efficient fighting unit, complete with a brave and determined crew. I could hardly take it in. She had turned over in less than twenty minutes after the bombs exploded and she sank early the next day. It seemed extraordinary that so many of us had got out of the ship, and I could only attribute this to our training, discipline and morale.

Bill Canning was later to record his memories of this terrible day: '*Broadsword*'s lowest ebb was reached on 25 May when, in company with HMS *Coventry* during anti-air operations north of Pebble Island, we were attacked late in the evening. It was not our day. Sea Wolf failed at a critical moment as the attack developed and, despite our combined efforts with Sea Dart, gun and an assortment of small arms, both ships were bombed at low level. The upshot is well documented: *Broadsword* survived while *Coventry* was lost.

'These were moments of great anguish, but my recollections remain clear. We strove to sort ourselves out and to prepare for another attack against the haunting knowledge that the *Coventry* survivors had abandoned ship. [But] how could this possibly have happened? Had I given *Coventry* enough help and direction? Indeed, in the heat of the moment, I even gained the impression, quite falsely, that my ship was trimming by the stern following the bomb strike aft. Among the many reports flooding into the ops room during this quite brief incident, there was one I shall never forget. It was a very controlled statement from my officer-of-the-watch. His words were simply, "*Coventry* has blown up."'

But if the day had been a disaster for *Coventry*, it had also been one for *Atlantic Conveyor*, which was later sunk well to the north of the Islands by an Exocet launched from an air-to-air-refuelled Super Étendard. Twelve men were lost. The ship was bringing Chinook and Wessex troop-carrying helicopters, a large quantity of steel planking for constructing an airstrip ashore for the Harriers and many other vital stores: the loss of such a valuable cargo was to have serious consequences for the land battle. Fortunately, the replacement Harriers, also a part of the cargo, had flown off earlier.

The loss of *Coventry* and *Atlantic Conveyor* shook both the Task Force and the country. Yet we soon realized that the air battle had largely been won on 25 May, and that this had been the enemy's final, desperate fling at us. Morale among the enemy aircrew was suffering badly and it really was only the second eleven left now: no more of our ships would be lost. A Royal Marine Commando, who was ashore when he heard we had been hit, remarked: 'Thank God for good old *Coventry*; if it wasn't for her it would have been us.' He made the point well.

Speaking after she heard the news, Mrs Thatcher had said: 'Despite these grievous losses, neither our resolve nor our confidence is weakened.' She later confided that this had been her worst night of the war, and there was a sombre mood in the Commons the next day when the Prime Minister addressed the House.

'Our fighting men,' she said, 'are engaged in one of the most remarkable military operations of modern times. In a series of measured steps, our forces have tightened their grip of the Falkland Islands.' Then, after paying tribute to *Coventry* and *Atlantic Conveyor*, she added: 'We do not yet know the number of casualties, but our hearts go out to all the families who had men in those ships. We in Britain know the reality of war. We know its hazards and its dangers. We know the task which faces our fighting men. They are now established on the Falkland Islands with all the necessary supplies, and although they are faced with formidable problems, in difficult terrain, with a hostile climate, their morale is high.'

I later read an account of 25 May which suggested that, after the earlier attacks had been fought off and the ships had suffered no damage, a cautious belief spread through the fleet that the Argentinian Air Force might well have shot its last bolt. Consequently, *Atlantic Conveyor* was ordered to set course for San Carlos Water. The plan was that she should anchor in the bay all night while her valuable goods were unloaded into a waiting flotilla of landing craft. We, too, had hoped that the attacks were over and looked forward to other ships relieving us in our sacrificial role the next day. But in reality, about 400 miles away to the west, the cream of what was left of the enemy air force was receiving last-minute instructions.

The Skyhawks were to fly high for the first half of the journey to conserve fuel and then drop down close to sea level. They were to concentrate on just a single ship – the one which was nearest and which their colleagues had spotted earlier: *Coventry*. They were ordered to head for the uninhabited westernmost edge of the Falklands and then to hop from the Jason Islands, Carcass Island, Saunders Island and, finally, Pebble Island before swinging left towards the open sea to launch their attack. The Argentinians knew well that our radar would be easily confused by the clutter created from land contacts, so they reasoned that if their aircraft spent as much time over land as possible, they might just get through. As the sun began to sink over the horizon, four Skyhawks were finally ordered to take off as these were the aircraft thought to stand the best chance of slipping through undetected. The assumption was correct. The first we knew was when four blips showed up on our radar screens only five miles and a few seconds away. It was too late and the bombs rained down. The attack had been both meticulously planned and courageously executed, although the latter came as no surprise. Even at the time, we admired the Argentinian pilots for their dash and daring. To us, they were Fangios of the air.

Commodore Clapp, the commander of the Amphibious Task Group, later wrote: 'When *Coventry* was sunk, my heart was in my mouth that we might not be able to hold on in the naval sense. The Royal Marines and Paras appeared to be unharmed, but I still needed several more days to unload. I was beginning to worry about getting into a position where the land force could not be built up sufficiently to take Port Stanley and where we had insufficient ships to support them. But thank heavens, it never came to that. If the rate of attrition through air strikes on the first day had continued, I think we would have been very worried indeed.'

Yet the choice of San Carlos Water as the site for the landings was inspired: it was sufficiently landlocked to allow small boats to load and unload at any time and the hills around it would hamper air attack. We also achieved complete surprise and all the troops were able to get ashore by dawn on the first morning without a shot being fired. The unloading of stores and equipment then went ahead at pace and after 25 May the remainder of this part of the operation was largely unhindered by attacks from the air. The last troops to land, between 1 and 2 June, were men of the Fifth Infantry Brigade under the command of Brigadier Tony Wilson, consisting of the Second Scots Guards, First Welsh Guards and First/Seventh Gurkha Rifles. The assault force was now complete, and we had just, although only just, managed to hold the balance against the enemy air force.

The Iron Duke's words after Waterloo – 'The nearest run thing you ever saw in your life' – seemed all too appropriate, even if Wellington had been speaking of a few confused hours of cannon fire, cavalry charges and close-in fighting with musket and bayonet, whereas we had endured nearly four weeks of war and five ship losses. The Commander-in-Chief and the Prime Minister had been walking a high wire all this time. An Exocet could, at any stage, have disabled or, worse, sunk *Hermes*, *Invincible* or even *Canberra*. (*Hermes* was, after all, only four miles away from *Atlantic Conveyor* when the latter was hit.) The enemy's bombs could, from the outset, have been correctly fused for the low-level attacks our ships' missile systems had forced him to make. And his air forces could have kept up their attacks on our own hard-pressed amphibious forces at San Carlos after D-Day, when *Ardent* was sunk and four other frigates badly damaged. (Instead, they inexplicably allowed us twenty-four hours' respite.) The margin between victory and humiliating defeat had always been the narrowest.

As it was, on 26 May, the first of the British forces were ready to move from the beachhead and Brigadier Julian Thompson of the Royal Marines gave the order for the three Royal Marine Commandos, 40, 42 and 45, and the Second and Third Battalions, the Parachute Regiment, to begin their advance inland. They were to march, carrying as much equipment as they could bear, across exceptionally difficult terrain in appalling weather and fight their way to Stanley. I doubt any other soldiers in the world could have done this, and of all the troops, the Marines and the Paras were the best trained for the job. *Coventry*'s exploits had been all about making this advance on land possible – and even if we had now paid the heaviest price, we knew it had not been in vain.

CHAPTER 11

DAY'S END

The sun had set and darkness now descended on what was left of 25 May. It was a cold and black night. I was winched up from *Broadsword* into a helicopter and taken to RFA *Fort Austin* in San Carlos Water. Naturally, I was a little nervous about being in Bomb Alley but reckoned that nightfall would have put a stop to any air attacks. The bulk of my ship's company were taken to *Fort Austin* by boat. As the boats pulled away from *Broadsword*, the *Coventry* survivors raised three loud cheers in heartfelt thanks to the ship which had both come to their rescue and looked after them so well.

Dean Webster, a weapons electrician in *Broadsword*, wrote to me later and described the scene: 'It was sad to see the *Coventry* go down. It seemed to be surreal, the sky was blue and seagulls soaring round, it just didn't seem right. Later that evening, I helped some of the chaps up to the side of the hangar to where the ladder was down and a boat waiting. It was pitch black but I remember the cheers for *Broadsword* as the boat disappeared in the night. That day will stay with me for the rest of my life.' Bill Canning was also to recall those cheers, although for him they had had an even deeper resonance: 'While very moving, this generous act of cheering *Broadsword* seemed only to accentuate the sense of failure harboured in my subconscious.'

Broadsword was a wonderful ship to work with, as she amply demonstrated by carrying out our rescue so resourcefully and efficiently, at the end of a long day and while still licking her own wounds. (As well as suffering damage to her flight deck and helicopter from a bomb, she too had been strafed by heavy cannon fire.) Bill Canning clearly inspired his men and was always a tower of strength to me. Both he and his ship's company may have felt they had let me down because they were there to defend me with *Broadsword*'s missiles, but I never thought that at all. When he was interviewed on the day he returned to England, Bill was to say: 'Our worst moment was when *Coventry* was sunk almost alongside us. In a way we had failed to stop her being sunk.' He minded so much. Although I was following the tactics we had agreed, all that each ship could do in the circumstances was to fight for its life and try to survive.

In due course, I was taken to see the captain of *Fort Austin*, Commodore Sam Dunlop. Sam was a kind and genial soul as well as a vastly experienced sea captain. We sat down in his cabin and had a much-needed glass of brandy together. There wasn't a great deal to say, and I must have looked a sorry sight. None the less, he went on to tell me of the attack on *Atlantic Conveyor*, which came to me as a bolt from the blue. We then listened to the ten o'clock news and heard the BBC World Service announce that a destroyer had been sunk. This was, if anything, even more of a shock: the ship's name was not mentioned, and I had to think long and hard before I realized they were referring to *Coventry* – my ship. I still couldn't believe it.

That night, I sent D a telegram which said simply, 'Safe and well'. The next day, feeling a little more chatty, I sent another: 'Relax completely am alive and very well back quite soon.' In the meantime, I was to sleep, or rather try to sleep, in a large, comfortable bed which could not have been a greater contrast to the solid and narrow warship bunk I was used to. I cannot say I enjoyed the experience: now that I was no longer buoyed up by the flow of adrenalin or the responsibilities of command, the first effects of shock were taking hold. When I retired to bed, I began to shake uncontrollably from cold and had to ask for several blankets to be piled on top of me; I also began to experience breathing difficulties and coughed up a considerable amount of a black, tar-like substance.

By now, most of my ship's company had arrived in *Fort Austin* and were also being very well looked after. I began to learn who had survived and who was missing. We carried out a roll call and listened to statements from witnesses, and began to write down names and details. The first lieutenant was found to be missing so Mike O'Connell, who took over his duties, now looked after the ship's company as best he could. His leadership would do much to restore morale and some cheerfulness to the bewildered ship's company. He came and saw me with the ship's doctor, Surgeon Lieutenant-Commander Oliver Howard, and they told me all they knew about events so far. I was distraught at this stage and they did their best to console me. The doctor gave me an injection of cortisone which eased my breathing. It was now a question of signalling the names of those who were lost to the

Commander-in-Chief so that next of kin could be informed. Suffice to say, it was a miserable time.

It was also, to say the least, a miserable time for our families back home. They knew a destroyer had been sunk – but which one? The First Sea Lord later acknowledged the error made in not announcing the name of the ship in the initial broadcast: it would obviously have been better to have confined the worry to some three hundred sailors' next of kin, rather than extend it to many thousands'. As far as D was concerned, she was, like everyone else, completely in the dark; and when she was finally informed that the ship was *Coventry*, she had to wait several more hours before she knew whether or not I had survived. Then, of course, she had to help care for some of the bereaved families who had just been told they had lost their husbands or sons. It was far worse for her than for me. At least I knew I was alive.

It was only when I returned to England and met Captain Michael Layard, the senior naval officer in *Atlantic Conveyor*, that I learnt the full story of her sorry end. Only twenty minutes after the Exocet had hit, it was clear that the ship was doomed, and both Captain North, who was in command, and Michael Layard concluded that it had to be abandoned. Ian North was the last to leave, with Michael climbing down the ship's side just below him. The side was glowing red in places and the paint peeling off. 'The descent seemed interminable,' he recalled, 'the more so as pieces of shrapnel from the explosions inside the ship were coming out through the side and singing past my ears. Added to which, I was half expecting that she and I would blow up at any second.'

Both Ian North and Michael Layard dropped into the sea and

were together to begin with, but they soon found themselves sucked in under the rounded section of the stern, and as it rose and fell in the swell, they were pushed underwater. They survived a few duckings and buffetings but it was definitely time to get to a life-raft. Michael recalled: 'My last sight of Ian, that dear old friend, was as I gave him a strong shove in the small of the back for the nearest life-raft. I then went under again and thought my number was really up this time and when, after what seemed a lifetime, I broke the surface again, the scene was quite different. There was no sign of Ian. I swam to a life-raft and was hauled in. It was several minutes before I was able to take much interest in my surroundings as I coughed up large quantities of sea out of my lungs. When I did, it was nearly dark except for *Atlantic Conveyor* glowing like a beacon beside us.' Ian North was, by all accounts, a wonderful man. He had served in the Merchant Navy in the Second World War, but his physical condition in his later years was such that he was unable to withstand such terrible treatment in the icy waters of the South Atlantic.

Captain North's ship's company had much the same experience as mine of having to survive in the cold water before being able to board a life-raft and find eventual safety. As it turned out, we were the only two ships in the Task Force that had to swim for our lives. The officers and men of the other ships that were lost were taken off by other vessels that came alongside, thus enabling them to keep their feet more or less dry. It is always traumatic to have to abandon a ship, whatever the means of leaving, but there is something particularly distressing about abandoning a trusted friend – the ship – to its fate by jumping over the side. Once you are in the water, another ordeal begins and survival remains far from certain: the trauma suffered by survivors must certainly have been greater among those who had to struggle in the water to save themselves before they were rescued. When I joined the Navy at Dartmouth, we all had to prove our swimming abilities by swimming two lengths of the pool in a boiler suit. I could see the sense of that now, even if I had not before.

D thought it was better not to tell Miranda and Alice that the ship had been sunk until she had heard whether I had survived, and so she took them off to school in the morning as usual but forgot to inform the teachers. The school, meanwhile, had heard the news and was naturally concerned for the girls. One teacher came up to Miranda and asked her how she was. Miranda, always rather anxious about her health as a child, was enchanted by this sudden interest in her well-being and replied, 'I'm very well thank you, apart from a little sniffle!' The teachers soon realized the situation and let them both get on with their day; D was able to tell the girls when they returned that afternoon that the ship had been sunk but that I was safe. Alice was unable to fully comprehend the news and asked if she could still go and spend the night with a friend, which she did. Miranda, on the other hand, sat down, went very red in the face and kept repeating, 'Oh dear, oh dear, poor Daddy, oh dear.'

Fort Austin sailed from San Carlos Water in the early hours of 26 May to rejoin the Battle Group to the east. The following day, we all transferred to RFA *Stromness* for the passage to South Georgia. *Stromness*, a 17,000-ton stores ship, was converted to carry Royal Marines and had brought 400 of them down to the South Atlantic, along with stores of all kinds filling every available space. My ship's company were to occupy the spaces left by the Marines, now setting out on their way to Stanley. At South Georgia, we would meet up with the *QE2* and embark in her for the passage home to the UK. *QE2*, with luxury fittings temporarily removed and helicopter flight decks constructed forward and aft, had transported over 3,000 troops at 28 knots to the battle zone. Her size, her renown and her precious cargo all made her a prime target, but she evaded all attacks. She had been converted for her new role at astonishing speed: one week she was the world's finest cruise liner, the next the world's greatest and fastest troopship.

CHAPTER 12

BRAVE DEEDS

While in *Fort Austin*, I received a signal from the Commander-in-Chief, Admiral Fieldhouse: 'The sad loss of your ship and your shipmates will be hard to bear for you all, but I want you and your ship's company to know that we are all proud of the magnificent fight you put up. You made an important contribution to the battle. Well done.' Later, when I was in *Stromness*, Sandy Woodward signalled me: 'Unusually, words nearly fail me. So sad to see a good ship and so many good men go: but I am glad to see so many survive. Go home now and sharpen up the second eleven, they look likely to be needed.'

I detected in that last sentence the seriousness of the loss of both *Coventry* and *Atlantic Conveyor*. So much had depended on these two ships, and Sandy Woodward must now have been wondering whether he really could bring off a victory. At least he knew that there was now only one Exocet missile left in the Argentinian armoury. For my part, I was heartened by these signals; to know that our contribution was recognized and valued took away a little of the pain. In the meantime, we began slowly to piece together events after the attack on *Coventry*. Many of the ship's company, it became clear, had performed brave deeds.

Between decks, two chief petty officers, Alan Fazackerley and David Rumsey, had on their own initiative revisited smoke-filled compartments to ensure that anyone still alive was got out of the ship, and they did this despite the fact the ship was listing dangerously and everyone else was now on the upper deck. Alan Fazackerley found a senior rating, Chief Petty Officer Alan Estcourt, unconscious, his clothes alight, slumped over a hatch above the after engine room and in imminent danger of falling back into the blazing compartment. He quenched the flames, took the senior rating to the after first-aid post and thence to the upper deck, saving his life. Alan Estcourt had been the last out of the after engine room as the port-side forward bulkhead ruptured, allowing a fireball to blast through the machinery space, which then quickly became smoke-logged.

Disregarding the ever-increasing hazards and rapidly diminishing chances of his own survival, Alan Fazackerley again went forward between decks, checking compartments for damage and signs of life. He was finally stopped at the junior ratings' dining room but was still able to see the extensive damage under the layers of smoke. He was seriously affected by this smoke but managed to return to the after-section base, now abandoned, and conducted a final search of previously inhabited spaces before moving to the upper deck. Here he joined Chief Petty Officer Derek Kimber in attending to the badly injured 'Eli' Ellis, lowering him into the water near a life-raft.

David Rumsey saved the lives of the two trapped and frightened young ratings in the transmitter equipment office close to the bomb hole and fire in the port passageway. He heard their agitated shouts for help, calmed them down, guided them painstakingly past the bomb damage and saw them to the upper deck. He then continued his search, quite alone, and by wriggling along on his stomach to keep below the layers of suffocating smoke, looked into several spaces for survivors before saving himself and swimming to a life-raft. He was probably one of the last ratings to leave the ship. Once in a life-raft which, like many, was grossly overloaded, he took charge of it, ensuring that shocked and injured survivors were properly looked after. He, with the help of Chief Petty Officer Charlie Findlay, contributed much towards the survival of some forty people.

Charlie Findlay, a tall and imposing man, had been closed up at his action station in the gyro compass room, adjacent to the computer room, and was immediately confronted with huge damage and water flooding in. He carried out a damage assessment, made a report and cleared out all personnel; only when the water was chest-high did he secure the watertight door and make for the upper deck. Several routes to this were blocked by buckled doors, ruptured decks and fallen furniture, but he eventually escaped through thick smoke and swam to a life-raft. But he did not stay here long because he saw Chief Petty Officer Brian Mallinson in considerable difficulties in the water and in great pain. He got him into the raft, discovered he had an injury to his back and injected him with morphine to relieve the pain. He even left the raft again to help push it away from the ship's side. Charlie Findlay was both a brave man and an outstanding leader.

There were a number of ratings below decks who were

injured, confused and disorientated by shock as a result of the explosions and would not have been able to get to the upper deck and to safety on their own. They were all rescued by courageous colleagues in the most frightening conditions of fire, smoke, broken ladders and a rapidly heeling ship. Leading Seaman Brian Smith, who had already demonstrated his bravery in attempting to clear the jam in the port 20-mm gun in the face of cannon fire and bomb blast, on his own saved the lives of two men who were badly shocked. One was Missileman Malcolm Rutherford, whom he helped over the side and into the water; the other was Sergeant Bill Baker, the RAF interpreter, who had lost his survival suit and could not have been more unused to the situation in which he now found himself. Brian Smith went in search of another suit and then saw the sergeant down the side and into the water, where he inflated his lifejacket and helped him swim to a life-raft.

The men in the life-raft that had been punctured when sucked into the overhanging bow of the ship ended up back in the water. The injured, some badly burnt and unable to swim, were held up above the sea by their colleagues until helicopters arrived and lifted them to safety. Other sailors, some injured and some without lifejackets or even survival suits, were succumbing to the cold water and cramp and were unable to reach life-rafts. They, too, were rescued by their colleagues and saved from drowning.

Sub-Lieutenant Andy Moll had already made a significant contribution to our successes in the air battle. He now showed considerable courage while in the water clinging to the outside of a life-raft. He noticed Radio Operator Fred Kelly was in difficulty: his lifejacket was split and he was in a state of panic.

Andy Moll left the relative safety of his hold on the life-raft and swam to recover Kelly, who was eventually pulled into the raft. This selfless act saved the radio operator from drowning.

A junior rating in the forward engine room, hearing a loud thump, looked around to see a bomb which had ripped into the compartment not far from where he was standing. He did not run, but went to a nearby telephone, reported the fact to the damage-control headquarters, described the bomb, the whereabouts of the gaping holes in the ship's structure and the nature of the damage to machinery. The bomb then blew up as he was still talking. Miraculously, he was shielded from the blast by machinery and survived. Four others were killed outright, however, among them Marine Engineer Artificer Paul Callus. Paul, such a likeable and capable engineer, was on board to complete his training and had plans to leave the Navy and emigrate with his American wife Cindy to the USA.

Lieutenant Chris Pollard, who was directing the close-range guns from the exposed position of the bridge wings, declined to duck for cover as the enemy aircraft closed at eye level and one of them strafed the ship with cannon fire. He then ordered the gun crews to stay at their posts and keep firing, which they did without question. Able Seaman Stephen Ingleby, manning the starboard 20-mm gun, had continued to engage aircraft with no thought for his own safety and achieved some hits on at least one; two others had turned away as a result of the barrage of fire. The gun crews remained at their posts, even after the ship began to list steeply, in case of another attack. Eventually, they were ordered to join the rest of the ship's company in abandoning ship.

Lieutenant-Commander Rob Hamilton later wrote of this

final, desperate day: 'It was remarkable that so many people kept their cool under such extreme circumstances – particularly those who went to make sure the sickbay, the tiller flat and other spaces got the message to abandon ship. Three times a leading seaman and two able seamen went into the devastated operations room to make sure everyone got out.

'One of my own strongest memories is of a sailor in *Broadsword*. I was taken down to 2 deck and stripped of my wet clothes. I was pushed into the wardroom, where the doctor looked me up and down and said nothing, causing me to wonder whether I was past help. I then found myself standing in front of the chaplain, who, like the doctor, said nothing, at which point I really did begin to think I was past all help. I was then pushed out of the other door where a sailor was waiting with a blanket. He quickly put the blanket over my shoulders and his arm around my waist and said, "Don't you worry about a thing, sunshine, you come with me." At that moment I ceased to worry about being the marine engineer officer of HMS *Coventry*.'

In due course, we were able to count the missing, whom we had to presume were dead. The total was nineteen. Nearly all were killed instantly by the blast of the bombs in the computer room, dining room, forward engine room and technical office. However, Kyu Ben Kwo, the laundryman from Hong Kong, died in the water on leaving the ship and we learnt later that he had a heart condition which would have precipitated his death. For a time there was a mystery surrounding the loss of the first lieutenant, Glen Robinson-Moltke, and I did not discover until I was back in England that he had not been killed directly by the bomb explosions. He had been in the damage-control head-quarters when the second bomb exploded and was severely shaken and concussed by the blast. He had to be pulled to his feet and directed to the upper deck, where he was observed to be considerably confused. He was seen helping someone to leave the ship but when he himself slid over the side, barely conscious, he hit his head on the protruding stabilizer and almost certainly broke his neck. He was never seen again. He had been brave to the last.

Apart from Glen, the only other officer killed was Rod Heath, who had so much to do with the success of Sea Dart. It was Rod, of course, that I had talked to on the bridge and thanked for his excellent work as I stood by the hatch before going down to the operations room for the last time. I was very saddened by the deaths of these two first-class officers. I was sad, too, that cook Ian Turnbull, a volunteer from *Aurora* who had become an enthusiastic member of the ship's company, had not survived.

Although we were now safely on board *Stromness*, we were all feeling sorry for ourselves, myself more than most. I simply could not avoid the overwhelming feeling that, as their captain, I had let my people down, and although they were my comrades-in-arms, I did not find it at all easy to be with the officers or men. This may seem odd as I had been with them in the ship through everything. But there was a difference: on board I had been invested with the captain's authority and lived apart. Now, like the rest, I was just a passenger in someone else's ship, and I felt out of place with no responsibility. I think I also felt vulnerable and I probably worried about what people thought of me: I was nervous of being drawn into a conversation about what had happened on our last day in case I heard some disturbing evidence that might have made me feel even more to blame than I already did. It took me some time, I must admit, to get over all this. It was, if you like, a sort of vicious emotional circle. The fact that I so admired the ship's company for both their loyalty to me and the way they had performed in very difficult situations only made me feel even more upset for having put them through these ordeals, and, in the process, for causing loss of life. After all, the prime responsibility of a commanding officer is for the well-being and safety of his crew.

Besides, I was looking like nothing on earth. Some flamazine cream was put on my face which formed a scab over the flash burns and hastened the healing process underneath; while my injuries were not at all serious or painful, I was none the less made to appear pretty awful for a week or two. I preferred, therefore, to recuperate slowly on my own in the confines of the comfortable cabin I was provided with, and this took me out of circulation with the ship's company. The captain of *Stromness*, Barry Dickinson, told me later that he thought of removing the mirror in the bathroom so that I wouldn't be able to see my face.

Not everything was doom and gloom, though. It was while I was in *Stromness* that my dream about my twin brother Robert suddenly came back to me. I was wide awake at the time, but everything seemed just as vivid as when I had first dreamt it on the eve of our sinking. In fact, it all returned with such surprising force and clarity I realized at once that it had been my brother who had saved me, and that it had been with his guidance that I had walked, almost unconsciously, out of the inferno of the operations room to safety. The complete void in my recollection between preparing myself to die one moment and being alert and safe the next had been explained. I have always felt that my brother is around somewhere as I journey through life, and this only confirmed it. Even now, whenever I choose to think about that dream, it still returns with the same unchanging clarity.

There was also the fact that, on our arrival on board, we had received a large batch of mail, which naturally cheered everyone up, myself included. Lieutenant-Commander Tim Fletcher, *Coventry*'s supply officer, wrote in his diary: 'By sympathetic planning or coincidence, our mail was waiting for us in *Stromness*. My personal letters from my family touched me very deeply and were a most effective balance to the events of the previous forty-eight hours.' His experience was shared by most of us, although letters telling of all the worries at home and the fears for our safety somehow only highlighted the traumatic times we had just lived through and brought many tears to the eye.

It was a strange coincidence that we should take passage in *Stromness* as she had spent a long period in company with *Coventry* during her deployment to the Far East in 1980. As the RFA was enjoying a stay of execution before being sold to the United States Navy, *Coventry*'s ship's crest, which had been presented to *Stromness* during that previous deployment, was formally returned to me before we left the ship as a memento of happier times. I have it to this day.

Inevitably, as I was not being seen around, people began to worry about me. One sailor, in an account of his time on board *Stromness*, wrote: 'We were becoming more and more concerned about the skipper. There were rumours abounding that he had been badly burnt and that he was blaming himself for the loss of *Coventry*. We wanted to see him to let him know that we didn't hold him responsible at all. My morale and that of my friends was given a great boost when we saw him up and about.'

Master-at-Arms Gerry Gilbert had, in fact, approached me and eventually persuaded me to be more visible. As you can imagine, such displays of concern were infinitely heartening to a captain who had just lost his ship: it made me feel immensely humble and merely intensified my regard and respect for my ship's company. I have read many books of people's war experiences when leaders in battle often express their love for their men. Love might not sound like the right word, but in the context of war, when you have seen your men perform fearlessly and unselfishly for the ship, or the regiment, then it is definitely the right word. I did love my men for all that they did, and for what they did for me. There can be no bond closer than that between men who have fought side by side in battle.

As it was, on the first day, very shortly after we arrived on board *Stromness*, one of the cooks from *Coventry*, a leading hand, had come into my cabin quite unannounced and said that he was glad to see I had survived and was safe, and he had held my hand. I, in my turn, had said I was glad to see him and then he left. Nothing more had needed to be said. Later, I was again to be very touched whenever some of my sailors came to visit me in my cabin, just to have a chat and to make sure I was all right. These solicitous gestures spoke volumes, not so much about me but about the situation we now all found ourselves in. Despite being 'homeless', we remained a fiercely proud and loyal ship's company who would feel content and secure as long as we were together. Having fought together and survived together, it was always going to be hard for us to leave each other and go our separate ways. I felt this very strongly. Indeed, I was still very much regarded as the captain of *Coventry* and, even after our return, it would be a long time before some people were able to stop clinging to this belief.

The loss of a ship entails not only the loss of a sea-going home but the break-up of a community with all its personalities, customs, skills and trades. All this has simply gone. More than that, a proud tradition has gone too – like that of a regiment which has been disbanded. In our case, the greater naval tradition would go on but the particular tradition of *Coventry* would die until there was another ship of the name to take over and create its own, one which would embrace the achievements of her predecessor. I was finding all this very hard to accept. Furthermore, even though it was nothing compared to the loss of our shipmates, there was also the fact we had all lost valuable or precious personal possessions. This only added to the misery of being homeless.

Even now, a quarter of a century later, I cannot forget the brave people in my ship who fought so well. Nor can I forget those equally brave men who lost their lives. It was a rare experience for someone of my generation to be able to lead such men in battle. They will always remain my heroes, and I shall always have proud memories of a very gallant ship.

My mother wrote a letter to me on 27 May: 'We heard the final news of your safety when D rang me yesterday afternoon. I'd heard the night before of the sinking of a destroyer but no name till 1 p.m. news. I'd been listening all night and felt sure it was *Coventry* and I could 'see' you standing there on the ship. You'll feel so sad at the loss of your ship, but I think it is wonderful how so many are rescued in these appalling conditions – and I hear you shot down several aircraft. It must have all been a terrible and terrifying experience, but you will be a comfort and a rock to your men as you all recover and pick up these strange threads of life again. D is being marvellous . . . Everybody here has been so kind and all the papers have your photograph.'

After two or three days in *Stromness*, we arrived in Grytviken, South Georgia, where we transferred to the *QE2* for the passage home. The sight of those majestic glacial mountains, in hues of blue, green and white, rising out of the translucent pale green sea was extraordinary; I have never seen a more beautiful landscape. It quite literally took your breath away: as I stepped out on deck to go to the waiting boat, I felt an icy blast of air on my face despite a complete absence of any wind, and the chill went deep into my bones. The place was magnificent but also eerily forbidding.

I was welcomed on board the *QE2* by the senior Royal Navy officer, Captain Jimmy James, who was serving on board as a liaison officer for the duration of the conflict. I was also to meet Captain Nick Barker of *Endurance*, whose ship was in the harbour at the time. I later met the master of the ship, Captain Peter Jackson, who made me feel at home straight away and whose officers and crew looked after us all so well and so sympathetically. I was shown to the Queen Elizabeth suite, one of the first-class cabins, complete with antique furniture, a private balcony, a bar and en suite bathroom. I wish I could have enjoyed it, but few of us were able to appreciate our luxurious surroundings. My ship's company was duly joined by those of *Ardent* and *Antelope*, whose commanding officers Alan West and Nick Tobin now became my travelling companions. As soon as everyone was embarked, we set sail for home.

Commanders West and Tobin were courageous men who took their ships into Falkland Sound where the threat from the air was at its greatest. They were there to protect the amphibious force at a crucial stage in the landings and they did so by being conspicuously positioned in open water to attract and take on the enemy in the air. Both ships were soon overwhelmed and fatally damaged but not before putting up a stiff fight. Nick I had known as a student in my syndicate at the Staff College. But Alan I hardly knew, although our ships had exercised together briefly at one time off Portland under the auspices of the Flag Officer Sea Training. He later rose to the highest ranks in the Navy, becoming the First Sea Lord in 2002, and is now retired.

As the final leg of our journey began, our thoughts not only turned to our families but also to those sailors we had left behind and their families. How cruel and hard it was going to be for them. Many of us now received further letters from home that had been diverted to *QE2* to await our arrival; these brought more emotional moments when reading about the anguish of loved ones. Inevitably, among the letters were some addressed to those who had died.

Able Seaman Mick Daniels later wrote: 'I think the sinking only hit me when we boarded *QE2* in South Georgia and once we had been allocated cabins, there were some tables with mail and parcels spread out on them. I could not help but stop and stare at the mail for some of our lost shipmates – it was hard not to be moved at the sight.'

Sub-Lieutenant Lee Jones recalled: 'Those days on passage were awful, truly dreadful. We had gone from a peak of activity and stress, living and working under continuous threat of attack for almost a month, to having nothing to do, absolutely nothing. As the injured members of the crew had been ferried to *Uganda*, we couldn't even establish with any certainty how many of our colleagues had been killed, and who they were. Few of us had any more than the clothes we were standing up in.'

At first, I lost track of time completely as I remained totally absorbed by all that had happened so recently. Everything passed by in a blur. Nor was I at this stage looking ahead to being at home. My mind was fixed on the war and the pain of loss. But I did at least think we were fortunate to have some time during the passage home which would enable us to adjust and gradually to focus more on both the present and the future. We had, I think, left South Georgia on 30 May, and we were due back in Southampton on 11 June.

I cannot remember exactly when I received D's letter sent on 28 May after she had learnt of the sinking of *Coventry* and of my survival; perhaps there was a mail delivery flown out to us as we passed Ascension Island. The letter was upsetting to read as it vividly told of the strains and anxieties D had been suffering. It brought home to me how brave she had been and how much of a tower of strength to so many of the *Coventry* families. And all this whilst she had also had to protect and reassure our children. For over two months, she had been alone, wondering and worrying about me and *Coventry* as well as shouldering the concerns of others. I had not had those strains and I had also always felt so much more in control of my own destiny. Looking back now, I think that my only real worry throughout had been that D would be worrying about me.

D wrote: 'The last three days have been an unbelievable nightmare – I cannot bear to think of what you must be going through at the loss of that beautiful ship, with Glen, Rod Heath and the other sailors. It must be the most devastating experience. Sam Salt so kindly looked in on his way back from Brize Norton yesterday to tell me how you would be feeling. He said you would feel like crying for the next month, and as he spoke tears came into his eyes. Of course, the only thing that mattered to me was to know that you were safe.

'Michael Gordon-Lennox [an officer serving on the C-in-C's staff at Northwood] rang me at 11.30 at night to say *Coventry* had been hit and I had to wait till 3.30 the next afternoon to hear if you were alive. I spent the night doing strange things like sorting out the children's clothes and making the spare room beds. *Coventry* families rang me all night but of course I had no news for them. Judy Barrow [the wife of *Glamorgan*'s captain] came and spent the whole day with me and was wonderful – answering the telephone, warding off the press and just being calm and down to earth.

'When Michael rang to say you were safe, it was the most wonderful moment I can remember – and I at once rang your mother: no need to describe her feelings. Letters, telegrams, flowers etc. pour in endlessly. Friends are overwhelmingly kind. They all feel deeply concerned for you – some arrived on the doorstep in tears and I had to send them away as I had no wish to be reduced to tears myself. In fact, I have been totally calm for two days, but today I feel quite dreadful. My heart goes out so much to dear Christine [Robinson-Moltke] and Jan [Heath] – and the other families. I've been with Christine a lot – she is quite incredibly brave – but at last this morning broke down when letters from Glen arrived – the first we've had. In one letter he said he knew he would probably not come out of this alive, and so he wrote it as a farewell letter.

'I won't embark on the whole trauma of how we were all told about *Coventry* and the long delays in telling relatives – there is no doubt going to be an almighty row about it.

'You feature in endless newspapers which I will keep and I eventually had to make a statement to the press, with Richard [Luce] here. It's so wonderful to get your telegram and letters today. I feel so wrung out and exhausted having somehow found myself keeping everyone else going throughout all this. The parents of sailors with whom I've been in touch over the last few weeks ring me from all over the country to tell me their sons are safe and how deeply relieved they are to hear you are safe too. It's really very moving – I feel they've all become friends – we've all been through so much together.

'You must be so proud of all the ship's company, as we all are of you. The tribute to *Coventry* in the House of Commons was glowing and there were tears in people's eyes. I gather you had done so well all day – shooting down planes – and were just overwhelmed at the end. Everyone tells me that you were the first Type 42 to use your missiles really successfully. I always knew you would do everything so well and if you had to go down, at least you have the comfort of knowing you went down in a moment of glory.

'The cities of Portsmouth and Coventry mourn deeply. Thousands send love, sympathy, understanding and every other kind of message – everyone feels for you deeply. This letter is so inadequate – but you know what I am feeling – deep relief and happiness that you are safe – and sharing the anguish and misery of the families of those who are lost. I pray you will soon be on your way home.'

Flags had hung at half-mast over the city of Coventry on 26

May as people remembered the ship and sailors who had become so much a part of their community. One woman, when interviewed, had said: 'It was like a family the people had adopted. The whole family was sitting on that ship and the heart of Coventry was there with them. The ship was something that was Coventry, even if it was on the other side of the world. Everyone feels as if a chunk of the city has been plucked out. I could see the sadness of the people's faces as they passed the news around. It was like the whole place was in mourning, as if it was a personal tragedy for each individual citizen.'

Later, Rob Hamilton was to write a short poem on the passage home:

> In the Cathedral three great nails once held
> Hearts of oak until in war they were felled
> In cruciform they found new life
> To guide men's hearts in peace and strife
> Now they mark the watery grave
> Of a ship and her men giving all to save.

Our cross of nails, that so tangible symbol of the ship's intimate ties with the city of Coventry, had remained in its place, defiant, until the end. It had not survived, but many of us had and for that at least we could be thankful.

CHAPTER 13

HEADING HOME

After the war, Sandy Woodward wrote in his memoirs, *One Hundred Days*:

The loss of HMS *Coventry*, the last of my original picket ships, weighed heavily upon me. I had lost an old and familiar friend. I stood once more alone in the glass-fronted Admiral's bridge on that desolate afternoon staring out over the cold Atlantic, watching the always busy deck of *Hermes* and cursing the world in general. It was still 25 May, as it had been, it seemed to me, for about the last thousand hours.

I gazed at the sea, and pondered the many times I had stood here before; times when I had searched my own soul, wondering whether I should send the quietly spoken David Hart Dyke into the most lethal spot on this most lethal southern ocean. Well, I suppose I had done it once too often and now the gallant *Coventry* was gone – small comfort for her captain to know that she had gone down fighting, in a manner which had conferred the greatest credit upon his crew and indeed had done his illustrious family proud.

Doubtless as I stood there, he was resting in *Broadsword*, alone as he will always be, with the terrible visions of the last moments of his ship, of the fires, of the screams of the burning men, of lost friends, of the darkness and the helplessness. I doubt if it will ever be entirely erased from his subconscious, though in moments of sadness he may perhaps find solace in the heroism and the selflessness demonstrated by the young men who fought with him, to the end. There is an aura of lasting, private glory about such disasters, understood, inevitably, only by those who were actually there.

As the *QE2* cruised homewards, I began slowly to come to terms with my loss. In this, I was aided greatly by the ship's company, who went out of their way to show sympathy and to help restore my spirits. I was rather far removed from the others in my smart cabin on one of the uppermost decks, but this never seemed to stop people coming to see me. It was so good to talk to them and find out their thoughts and feelings about their experiences in the war and in what directions they thought their lives might be going next. My own feelings for the ship's company remained very intense and this was to last for some time. The sadness of losing the ship and some of my people was profound. We somehow had not deserved to go down on that last fierce day of fighting. It was like falling at the last fence in the Grand National when well in the lead, but a million times worse.

My letter to D of 4 June made mention of my burns and told a little of my emotional state: 'Who would have thought I would be cruising on the *QE2* from South Georgia to Southampton? I escaped miraculously from the ship which sank in a few minutes after shooting down several aircraft, but I did get my face burnt by the flash of the exploding bomb – but not badly at all, only one layer in places was burnt off. The treatment is to cover the face with a thick cream which hardens and allows new skin to form underneath. So when all the scabbing has dropped off, I will be back to normal again. Thought I had better warn you in case you get a bit of a shock, and you can explain this to the children too. As you can imagine, I have been in a very emotional state mainly because the ship's company seem to worship me and don't want to leave me. It's been a heroic ship and the sailors nothing short of heroes. To have been the captain has been a momentous and unique experience. Everyone needed me to take them through the dangerous times and they now regard me as their saviour and the reason for them being alive now. More about this later, but it totally reduces me to tears.'

It is difficult to believe now that I should have expressed those feelings in a letter, but if nothing else it demonstrates how deeply I felt for those who had fought with me so bravely. They, clearly, felt much the same, as did their relatives. The petty officer who had given me the prayer and hauled me into a life-raft was Paddy Burke, a delightful Irishman and an excellent steward who looked after the wardroom impeccably. Shortly after I returned home, I received a gift of an ornament of a silver Irish setter from his parents along with a note: 'Thank you for our son. He is our number one sailor.' Those few words of thanks overflowed with meaning.

Most of my crew could still only think about the ship to which they felt they still belonged, and they continued to look to me as their captain. They clung to each other closely and, like me, could not yet quite believe the ship had gone. (Later, even after I had returned and had gone into Portsmouth dockyard, I found it hard to credit that the ship was not alongside the wall in her familiar berth.) However, as the days went by and people talked each other through their experiences, they began once again to look forward, accept their situation and become more themselves. For my part, I began at last to circulate around the ship and to join the other commanding officers and officers from all the ships when the opportunity arose. We were together for meals in the main dining room, and even though the food was five-star compared with our action menus in *Coventry*, I don't think many of us were yet in the mood to enjoy it much.

All members of the ship's company were asked to write down their experiences of the war while these were fresh in their minds and in particular to describe their part in the final action. As a report would have to be made later to the Commander-in-Chief on *Coventry*'s involvement in the war from beginning to end, including all the details of her last moments, a collection of personal stories and views would provide a sound basis for it. This was a good mind-clearing exercise as well as being therapeutic for some, as it helped them to talk about the bad moments and to put those behind them.

We were duly invited to submit claims for the personal possessions that we had lost and we all eventually got some financial compensation from the Navy, but it was a small amount for most people and fell well short of the true value of the lost items. (Someone did, though, receive compensation for a lawn-mower he had brought on board for repair.) Those that lived on board all the time, as opposed to those who were married and went home to families in the Portsmouth area, had had nearly all their worldly belongings with them. I, clearly, did not live on board, but I had none the less brought all my best clothes and clobber with me – suits, blazers, sports jacket, dinner jackets and every item of uniform. And there was also the matter of the bottle of rum still on the bridge.

I spent many hours walking around the decks of the *QE2*, lapping up any sun and feeling the restorative salt air on my face. The flash burns were healing quite quickly and my hands and wrists were soon restored to full use. The medical staff on board were very helpful and, towards the end of the journey, the scabs on my face were gently removed to reveal a reasonably normal face underneath. Patrick Hewetson, the doctor who did much to speed up my recovery, was an enjoyable companion and also something of a social animal. His invitation to one particularly memorable party read: 'Doctor Alan Kirwin and Doctor Patrick Hewetson invite you to a tincture at 6.30 pm on Monday 7 June on our helicopter deck. Wheelchairs at 8 pm.'

Such occasions were a great help in diverting our thoughts away from the recent past and getting us back to something approaching normality. One night, the three ships' companies and the crew of *QE2* enjoyed a very entertaining concert party or 'sods opera', as these events are known in the Navy. All kinds of musical and other talent came to the fore. The master of ceremonies was Chief Petty Officer Derek Kimber, a brave man from *Coventry*. Another *Coventry* man, Petty Officer Cook Leslie Kellett, took the first spot as a stand-up comic for ten minutes. His threat of blue jokes, amply fulfilled, fortunately failed to offend the female Cunard staff in the audience. Lieutenant Bert Ledingham gave a wonderful performance on the guitar to rousing applause. It was all very good fun, the first for some time for many of us, and it felt a very novel experience to be really laughing again.

Captain Jackson hosted a magnificent dinner early on in the trip for all the officers of the lost ships; this was Cunard's way of welcoming us formally on board and commending us for our efforts. We dined in splendour in the elegant first-class dining room at candlelit tables. I was unable to eat all the delicacies placed in front of me as my mouth and lips were still sore from burns, and so I remember the occasion not so much for the excellent food but more for the generosity of the gesture and the descriptions of the various courses printed on the menu. We had Melon with Westphalian Ham, Ascension; Crayfish Cocktail, Tristan de Cunha; Filet Steak, Garni QE2; Pommes Frites, Goose Green; Bombe, Port Stanley and Falkland Cheese Board. I forget exactly what the bombe consisted of, but I was only just able to appreciate the black humour of the description.

There was a distinctly more solemn occasion when I faced the assembled ship's company for the first time at a memorial service which we held for ourselves to remember our shipmates who had died. I devised and conducted the service which was simple and short: the Naval Prayer, two verses of 'Eternal Father, Strong to Save' and a lesson from the First Epistle to the Corinthians formed the central part of it. The lesson ended with the verses: 'For since by man came death, by man came also the resurrection of the dead. For as in Adam all die, even so in Christ shall all be made alive.' Towards the end of the service, the names of those lost were read out before we observed a two-minute silence. The nineteen names were printed on the back of the order of service sheet, the first time that they had been formally listed and seen by everyone. For many, myself included, this was a particularly emotional moment which made them all too aware of the extent of the tragedy and of those who had been killed. At the same time, I think it helped people to draw some sort of line and start looking ahead and getting their lives back on track.

I was able to telephone home when we got within reasonable range of England and talk with D. I knew it was going to be a complete surprise for her, and she duly answered with more than a hint of disbelief and excitement in her voice. I was a little apprehensive about telephoning as I wanted to sound strong and happy like my old self and not to give any indication of my still rather fragile state. I warned her about my burns, as I had already done in a letter, but said they were now well on their way to healing, and I ended on a positive note. She sounded very close and it was a thrill to hear her again, but I think the conversation made me nervous about going home: I knew I would have to put on a brave front to appear back to normal, something I quite clearly was not. For the time being, I felt secure in *QE2* and I sensed life would not be quite so easy back home, however much I really wanted to be there.

D wrote the day after my call, although I only received the letter on arrival in Southampton: 'It was such a wonderful surprise to hear you so clearly on the telephone – I could hardly believe it and your voice sounded so strong. There is so much to write and talk about – but it can now all wait until you get home. A moment I can hardly wait for – and just hope the wonderful weather lasts so you can sit in the peace and quiet of the garden. I feel it may be difficult for you when you are parted from the ship's company – as you've been through so much together, but I hope that life going on in the same old way at home will help.'

Miranda enclosed a letter along with D's: 'I loved your picture of everybody fighting with their guns. It is very sad about the ship being sunk. I was hoping you could record me playing my new pieces on the piano. But everything is lying at the bottom of the sea. Anyway, at least you are safe.'

D was absolutely right about the final, and unavoidable, parting of the ship's company when we got back. It would mean not only the end of *Coventry* but also the end of the comforting support of colleagues who had shared the same experiences and so knew how to listen and help. Once at home, we would have to get through the lingering shock and sadness largely on our own. It would be difficult, too, for some families to cope with their returning loved ones who had yet to recover.

The time came for me to address the ship's company for the last time, on the day before our arrival. This was, I think, the saddest and most difficult thing I have ever had to do. As I walked with Lieutenant-Commander Mike O'Connell up the few steps, still hidden from view, before turning the corner to face the assembled company from the centre of a stage, I struggled to contain my tears. What could you say to a ship's company still so bewildered and bereft of their ship for which they had sacrificed so much? I thanked them all from the bottom of my heart and expressed my deep admiration for all they had done, and I wished them good luck for the future.

After I had finished speaking, the youngest sailor on board presented me with an autograph book: on every page were personal messages, tributes and farewells from members of the ship's company. I had had no idea this was going to happen and was deeply touched. Then, again to my complete surprise, I was presented with a sword, borrowed for the occasion from *QE2*'s captain, Peter Jackson: it was handed to me with the promise that the ship's company would be purchasing me a new sword to replace the one I had lost with the ship. I could not help thinking that this was far more than I deserved, and I left them all feeling overwhelmingly sad.

Richard Luce had written to me on 8 June: 'What pleasure and relief it is for all of us to know that you are home on Friday – and safe. I am sure the return will be the most exciting of your life in terms of seeing your family again – but also emotional and strenuous when you do so against the background of having lost some of your splendid men and your ship. But we are all very proud of you and all your crew for serving your country so magnificently. D has been splendid – calm and so considerate of the families of your crew and especially those who died. You will be very proud of her and of the girls.'

D had certainly been splendid, as the Commander-in-Chief, Sir John Fieldhouse, acknowledged when he wrote to thank her for all her vitally morale-boosting work. A few weeks later, at a gathering of ex-*Coventry*s in the barracks at HMS *Nelson*, she was given an antique silver sugar castor in recognition of her efforts in helping the *Coventry* families both during the conflict and afterwards when, inevitably, she became even more closely involved with those who had lost sons or husbands. It was at this gathering that I was duly presented with my new sword. It still hangs proudly, together with my telescope, in a corner at home and on the inside of its handle are the words: 'Presented to Captain D. Hart Dyke MVO Royal Navy with the respect and admiration of the ship's company. HMS *Coventry*. Falkland Islands 1982.'

The Royal Yacht *Britannia* (left) greets *QE2* on her return to Southampton on 11 June 1982. *Coventry*'s ship's company is gathered on the foredeck of the liner *(Beken of Cowes)*

The author, his wife D and daughters Miranda and Alice outside Coventry Cathedral in September 1982 *(Birmingham Post & Mail)*

The author and D with Chief Petty Officer David Rumsey and his wife Carol following the presentation of the new sword in August 1982. Former members of *Coventry*'s crew are gathered behind *(Portsmouth Evening News)*

Dinner at No. 10 Downing Street, 11 October 1982. Admirals Fieldhouse and Woodard confer, sitting far left. The author stands end left in the nearer row *(Empics)*

Captains together at the keel
laying of the new *Coventry*
and *Sheffield*, 22 March 1984:
Sam Salt, 5′ 4″, author 6′ 2″

(Gordon Amory of Express Newspapers)

The author handing over the Cross
of Nails to the Bishop of Coventry,
the Right Reverend John Gibbs, for
safe-keeping in the Cathedral, March
1983. Councillor Eddie Weaver, the Lord
Mayor of Coventry, and the Dean look on

(Mirrorpix/Coventry Evening Telegraph)

Ex-*Coventry* men by the ship's memorial on Pebble Island, dedicated 26 March 1983. From left to right, CPO Fazackerley, MEM Phillips, MEM Lendrum, LMEM Welbury, CPO Day, CPO Crowe and Lieutenant Adams

The inscription on the base of the memorial on Pebble Island

Now, though, we were preparing for our return and naturally became very excited at the prospect of being reunited with our families. Sir John Fieldhouse flew out to *QE2* as we approached the entrance to the English Channel so as to be the first to welcome us home and to thank us for all that we had achieved. He spoke to Alan West of *Ardent*, Nick Tobin of *Antelope* and me in Peter Jackson's day cabin and congratulated us. He then addressed the ships' companies with generous praise, a gesture which was quite unexpected but greatly appreciated. For my part, I was still not at all convinced that either I or my ship deserved special attention. We had, after all, only done what we were paid to do. But I was now beginning to realize that we were likely to be receiving a huge welcome when we got to Southampton and not a little media attention.

Able Seaman Izzy Isaacs described the scene as we approached Southampton Water: 'The night before we docked in Southampton, we could see the lights on land. I was up early the next morning, as was everybody – we could see the cars lining the roads waiting and flashing their lights, both on the mainland and the Isle of Wight. There were a myriad of small boats which followed us into the harbour. The whole area seemed to be full of boats and people waving.' In fact, I met Isaacs in the lift on the way down to breakfast on that last morning. He had been one of the bosun's mates who had kept watch for many long hours when I, too, was on the bridge. Now we shook hands and wished each other good luck.

At breakfast, I saw John Humphrys of the BBC and other familiar-looking media faces. They had flown on board early to talk to selected people, me among them. I was also interviewed at a hastily convened press conference by a number of newspaper journalists. I told them that the country could be proud of *Coventry*'s ship's company, who had performed magnificently. I added that I would always have happy memories of a great ship and an immense admiration for all those who had served in her, especially for those who had contributed so much but would not be coming home – they would never be forgotten. As I left the conference, there was loud applause. It came, I noticed, from my sailors, loyal to the last.

As we steamed up the Channel on a calm summer's day, we met up with the royal yacht *Britannia*, escorted by the frigate *Londonderry*, and passed close by her as our ships' companies lined the decks and cheered Queen Elizabeth, the Queen Mother, who could be seen standing on the after-deck. She sent us a signal welcoming us home and congratulating us on our part in the war. It read: 'The deeds and valour of *Coventry*, *Ardent* and *Antelope* have been acclaimed throughout the land. I am proud to add my personal tribute.' I had, of course, served as the commander of *Britannia* for two years not long before taking command of *Coventry*, so it was a particular pleasure to see that magnificent vessel again.

Lieutenant-Commander Tim Fletcher later wrote of his feelings on this day: 'From the Needles onwards, the carnival atmosphere was enough to move the most phlegmatic of men. I was even able to sight my father in his yacht as he battled gallantly with the throng of boats off the River Hamble and, later, off the Ocean Terminal as *QE2* was turned prior to berthing.

'My thoughts, though, were inevitably with the two members of my department who had been killed in action, Stephen Dawson and Ian Turnbull. It was to be a privilege and an honour to meet their families and to witness their resilience and acceptance, without rancour, of the fate that had befallen their sons. I could only hope that, in filling in some of the details of the last minutes of *Coventry*, I would be able to give them some comfort.

'I was intensely proud to have served in *Coventry* during the conflict, where I believed we had made a significant contribution. I also knew that I would have felt cheated if, after eighteen years in the Royal Navy, I had not been able to play an active role in the most demanding challenge the Navy had to meet during my service. But I had not enjoyed war. Service life has plenty of good times, yet there is always the possibility of a payback – and the Falklands campaign was the largest payback of my career.'

I imagine many of my ship's company felt much the same. But there was nothing left to do now but to change into the makeshift uniforms which had been sent out to us and to prepare for the long-awaited return to England's shores. I had been at sea continuously since the end of March. I was not at all sure how I would cope with seeing D and my daughters again, and I was apprehensive about both this and being hurled into a life ashore in the full gaze of the media: I felt that I had really needed another week in *QE2* to continue my rehabilitation. But I was also conscious of my naval training, and of the expectations of the thousands who had gathered to welcome us home. So I put my shoulders back, held my head high and prepared to walk ashore as bravely as I could.

CHAPTER 14

COMING
TO TERMS

It was an extraordinary sight. The ship's company of *Coventry* left *QE2* to be welcomed by thousands of cheering people. As they stepped off the gangway on to the shore, they were taken aback to find they were walking along a red carpet between rows of loudly applauding VIPs and dignitaries. The red carpet led them into the Customs shed, where young girls ran up to each crew member and presented him with a single red rose. Somehow, everyone found their way to their families through the throng, and most were then driven home, where they could celebrate their safe return and perhaps even relax properly for the first time in weeks. They now no longer belonged to a ship or to a close-knit company of friends and shipmates, but they were lovingly embraced by their families, who would soon discover that their priorities were now much more balanced and their outlook on life more mature. Their time in *Coventry* at war had shaped – and was going to continue to shape – their characters more than anything else in their lives.

Radio Supervisor Sam MacFarlane later recalled his homecoming: 'The realization that these hundreds of boats, helicopters, and people were here to welcome us was a weird feeling. We had only done our job. As we rounded the corner to the Cunard berth, we saw the thousands of people and choked. After what seemed an eternity, a door opened down below on 5 deck, and we were invited to walk ashore to a tumultuous "Land of Hope and Glory", cheers, handshakes, well-dones, and a red rose. The first time I saw my wife and children, I knew we were really home, and cried, just a little; the realization of the fact that I might never have seen them again hit home like a sledgehammer.'

Able Seaman Richard Hopgood was equally relieved but also apprehensive: 'The sight of those thousands of people who had come to meet us was amazing, banners and bunting everywhere. It was impossible to look for your family, just a time to enjoy the atmosphere. It was great to be back on British soil, but the greatest joy was seeing family and loved ones. The journey from Southampton to Essex was quiet, people not knowing what to say. Once home, it was a round of meeting the family and friends. It was going to be strange to adapt to life again: we had been so long away, so much had happened, and we had had so much time to reflect – and now it was going to be trying to get back to normal, whatever that was.'

We all worried about returning to normality. We also knew full well that, if it was going to be hard for us, it was going to be harder for those at home who had lost sons or husbands. I was particularly struck by a letter – positive, unselfish and with no hint of self-pity – written by Brian Callus, the father of Paul and a retired naval officer himself, to Margaret Thatcher within a few days of the death of his son. He urged her to make sure the Falklands campaign was successfully completed so that Paul's sacrifice in *Coventry* should not be in vain, and he offered his support. He duly received a reply on headed paper from 10 Downing Street. It was dated 14 June – the day of the Argentinian surrender – and read as follows: 'Dear Commander Callus, Thank you so much for your letter. I know that nothing I say will make up for the loss of your son. But he gave his life for very important principles, and that will never be forgotten. I am determined that Argentina should not profit from its aggression, and your prayers and support mean a lot. With all my sympathies.' Added to this was a handwritten paragraph: 'And today we have received the news we have been waiting for and it is all due to men like Paul. A sad, but proud day for you.' There is now a magnolia planted in Paul's memory in the garden of the little Roman Catholic church in Emsworth, Hampshire, where he used to help serve mass.

Since 25 May 1982, I have learned a good deal about shock. Its most immediate effect is to render you incapable of appreciating what has really happened and thus largely unaware of the horrific experience you have been through. This is perhaps no bad thing – it is nature's way of shielding you until you have sufficiently recovered your strength. And I was certainly both cocooned by shock and insulated from reality for most of the long journey back to England. I was unsmiling, preoccupied with my thoughts and still emotional. Just like everyone else, I dreaded the time we would have to say our farewells. Of all our generation, only we could know what a fierce battle at sea in the missile age was really like, and just how it had been to leave a burning ship in the cold waters of the South Atlantic. In a way, I think we already knew that our memories of these traumatic events were never going to fade, and that we were only ever going to be able to talk easily about them with those who had been there. For you always need to talk about such things, even if the tears well up as you do so.

The process of recovery tends to set its own pace: there is not a great deal you can do to speed it up. That said, just as riders need to climb back on to a horse straight after a fall to restore their confidence, so you need to return to work, in whatever form, as quickly as you can after a major trauma: doing so will help you accumulate new experiences and put the past into perspective. Due allowance has, of course, always to be made for some who may need more time to recover. A sea-going admiral who endured the worst of the fighting in the Mediterranean in the Second World War had to be sent home: he had survived the blowing up of the battleship *Barham* after it had been torpedoed by a U-boat, but the Commander-in-Chief had noticed that he was very shaken and simply not himself any more. I know exactly how he felt: I would certainly not have been quite myself had I been asked to take command of another ship straight after being plucked from the water.

We all respond differently in these situations, but I found mere expressions of sympathy, however well intentioned, were not what I needed. What did help, though, was when people showed a genuine willingness to ask me about my experiences and then to listen as I talked about them. After all, the worst thing you can do when you are trying to come to terms with a major trauma is to bottle up your feelings: the longer you do so, the longer you will suffer in silence. Yet silence is not always self-inflicted. On my return, I was bewildered by the fact that some of my naval colleagues seemed reluctant to discuss the

Falklands conflict. Later, I came to realize that they felt awkward: they did not know quite what to say and anyway presumed I would not wish to be reminded of such painful events. Perhaps there was also an element of professional jealousy in their behaviour – a sense that they had wanted to be in the action themselves and so did not want to hear anything about it from me. But even though I now understand their reserve, I would have much preferred them to have been more forthcoming. As with a bereavement, it may be hard to find the right words, but it is always important to say something.

My own rehabilitation was to last some eighteen months. Over time, I became aware that I was gradually enjoying family and naval life much more and looking forward rather than back, and I daresay my superiors at Northwood, where I now worked as an adviser to the Commander-in-Chief, were happier with my productivity. Yet what I remember most distinctly is that one day, quite suddenly, I felt so much better about myself: I did so for no obvious reason, and I think I even chuckled to myself at the realization. It felt as though I had been relieved of a certain weight around me, and I knew then that I was back to being my old self. Up to this point, perhaps, people had been either too kind or too nervous to tell me that I was not all right; I might have thought I had returned to normal fairly soon after stepping ashore in Southampton, but in reality I was far from it.

In most respects, though, I had been extremely fortunate. A few members of my ship's company were to suffer for many years afterwards and some, who appeared to recover quickly, broke down subsequently several years later. Those who clung to the notion of the ship still existing and of me being their captain found it more difficult than most, as they were unable to strike out into a new life and put the past behind them. Reunions of former comrades can, of course, be a source of considerable comfort and may even become compelling later in life. Equally, they can sometimes have decidedly adverse effects on the state of mind of someone younger who is still dwelling on the past and seeking solace in reliving events that would otherwise be receding into distant memory, which is the best place for them.

Like a number of my sailors, Weapons Electrician Stephen Woolham lived in Coventry. Six years later, in 1988, he was still full of memories of *Coventry*'s last action but had at last come to terms with them. He recalled: 'I was down below. There were some dull thumps and noise like tearing of metal. I knew we had been hit. When it came to my turn to leave, I checked that nobody had been left behind in our compartment. I jumped into the sea. I got so cold that I had to be helped into a life-raft. Then the helicopters came to pick us up. For the first two years after that I had vivid nightmares and thought about shipmates we had lost. Now, though, the bad memories have faded and proud and happy ones are uppermost.' I myself never experienced nightmares or flashbacks, although I know that a number of my people did. Proud and happy memories are now uppermost in my mind, too. There are many others who feel much the same and say they have gained from their experiences.

Twelve former members of my ship's company were sent to serve in *Hermes* and on 25 May 1983 they arranged a special anniversary dinner for themselves on board to remember *Coventry* and their lost colleagues. They called it 'Pebble Island Night' and it was clearly a huge success. Among those present was Petty Officer Steward Mick Stuart, who sent me a letter and a photograph showing the twelve seated together around the lavishly laid table complete with candlesticks. 'Just to let you know,' he wrote, 'we ex-*Coventry*s had a great time on the evening of the 25 May. You and yours were very much in our thoughts. It was fortunate that the enclosed photographs were taken early on in the evening because things were somewhat blurred at the latter stages of the meal.' Comrades in arms are not easily split up and, finding themselves together again, these men felt a strong need to share their memories and experiences. For my part, it was a real pleasure to receive Mick Stuart's letter and see those familiar faces again.

Marine Engineer Mechanic Peter Richardson, who now runs a successful security business, wrote to me in 2001 after watching a television documentary on the sinking of the ship: 'The memories came flooding back, my heart sank and tears filled my eyes: although I was only seventeen, I will never forget the *Coventry* and the comradeship we all shared . . . Looking back, I feel privileged and proud to have served under you. Our respect for our captain was and will always be immense; only you made the closeness of the crew possible . . . The men who were lost and the captain who cared will always remain in my soul till the day I die; without doubt you made us all one big family . . . and to me HMS *Coventry* was you . . .'

I hesitate to quote from such letters when they focus on me, yet I do so because I think that, like so many others I have received, they say much more about the writer and his *Coventry* shipmates than they do about me. It was simply my job to provide strong leadership and to ensure my crew followed me willingly, whatever the hardships, and I found this could be more easily achieved by showing care and respect for them and by keeping them as well informed as I could about our situation.

Peter Richardson's letter speaks of a ship's company under pressure, facing danger day in, day out over a long period and all the while being obliged to perform their duties to the very best of their abilities. He had seen people remaining calm and steadfast while terrifying forces of destruction were at work all around them, sometimes at a distance, sometimes close and, finally, right inside the ship itself. This was not something he was ever going to forget.

None the less, it was astonishing that, after nearly twenty years, someone should have taken the trouble to track me down and write a letter that was still so full of feeling. But such is the collective strength of a ship's company when, *in extremis*, they are welded closely together in the interests of survival and they rally in support of their leader. They will do anything for each other, and they will perform miracles in fighting their ship, whatever the odds. The spirit and resilience, the stoicism and unselfishness, of a ship's company are truly astonishing when they are wound up for war. Peter Richardson would have observed all this too, at first hand, and as his letter amply demonstrated, he would have felt much the same himself.

In 2004, I heard from Leading Stores Assistant Andy Stewart. 'It was always a good ship,' he wrote. 'Whatever it was, we had it. You could feel it as soon as you walked over the gangway. You could feel it at sea. You could feel it in port. *Coventry* told me all about teamwork, told me all about loyalty, told me all about courage. It has given me a clear advantage in leadership capabilities. To have served in *Coventry* and to have worked alongside such a fine group of men was a privilege and a gift. To tell the truth, it was bigger than just doing it for England. It was being there for HMS *Coventry*.'

Peter Richardson and Andy Stewart are not alone in what they feel. And that is just how it should be. Former Able Seaman Mick Daniels, who in 1982 had been so frustrated in his desire to leave the Navy, could look back twenty-two years later: 'My time on board HMS *Coventry* was very happy and I was proud to have served on board her under your command. Nobody could have done any more or given any more on that fateful day. Everyone gave their all – and there's not a day goes by that I do not think of 25 May and our lost shipmates.'

It was in the First World War that the psychological damage which could be caused by post-traumatic stress disorder (PTSD), as it is now known, was initially recognized. It was then called shell shock because it was thought – wrongly as it turned out – that shockwaves from shells passing overhead damaged the brain, whereas the origins of the condition in fact lay in the terror of constant artillery fire. Today, PTSD affects those who find themselves on society's front line – fire-fighters, police and ambulance staff, for example – just as much as it does our servicemen fighting in Iraq, Afghanistan and elsewhere. One of its key symptoms is a sense of isolation: people just retreat within themselves. Guilt is often a very strong feature of the illness, and battle survivors may also feel that they have let their comrades down. It is an undoubtedly complex subject, but at least the lessons from two world wars and subsequent conflicts are there and the British armed forces are now taking them to heart.

I think I probably retreated a little within myself, but I never felt isolated. I continued to lead a normal social life, seeing and keeping up with family and friends. I cannot in all honesty say I ever felt guilty, although for a while I definitely did feel that I had let my comrades down. The strongest urge I had when I stepped ashore in Southampton was to tell the story of *Coventry* and its men because I felt I owed it to them to do so. How could they just be dispersed to other jobs in the Navy and never be heard of again after everything they had gone through?

As *QE2* had approached her berth, I had taken stock. My few belongings had been packed and I was now dressed in a working uniform, albeit not a particularly well-fitting one. Apart from the fact I had lost a good deal of weight, I believed I looked fit and well, despite the few scabs still marking my face from the burns. It was now sixteen days since we had been bombed and I had stumbled down the side of my ship into the icy seas of the South Atlantic, and this was a memory, among many others of that day, that remained far too fresh in my mind. At times, when I was preoccupied with these events, I was not great company, to say the least, and I was keenly aware that this was not going to make things any easier for either my wife or my daughters.

Then D, Miranda and Alice were shown up into my cabin – they must have been as nervous as I was, wondering what sort of person they would find. They all looked wonderful. We hugged and I shed some tears as I clung to D. She told the girls to go and have a look at my luxurious bathroom and its gold taps, something they did without question as they sensed that D and I needed a private moment to ourselves. Happiness and smiles quickly returned when the girls had seen enough of the bathroom and reappeared. We gathered ourselves together and made our way to the gangway: we were the first ashore. Television cameras whirred and microphones were thrust into our faces, but eventually we carved a way through the crowd and leapt into the shelter of our car.

I don't remember the journey to Petersfield or what we talked about during it. Miranda seemed rather quiet, but I was particularly conscious of Alice, who was looking at me very closely and wondering whether I was still the same person she remembered from twelve long weeks before. A month later, a note was found in the playroom which Alice had written only a day or so after my return. Her name and address were at the top of a small piece of lined paper and below them the words: 'I am 6 years old my daddy's ship sunk at the bottom of the Alantic ocon and he got burt and he came back on the QE2 I didnt dare to look at his face'.

There is something about the Navy and a life at sea that teaches you to carry out your duties efficiently and without fuss, whatever the situation. The sea itself, with all its dangers and uncertainties, instils a measure of humility and a broader sense of perspective. While I was entirely satisfied that I had done my duty to the best of my abilities and contributed something to the successes of the war, I was neither expecting to be thanked so personally by the British public, and nor, as I have said, did I think I was particularly deserving of such thanks. I was therefore genuinely taken aback to observe how Britain so admired its fighting men and celebrated their return. I knew that the country had believed in the war and how strongly it had supported us, but I was largely unprepared for the adulation we received. I only wanted to go home quietly, fade into the background and be left to enjoy family life.

I was indeed able to enjoy family life again, and it was absolute bliss; however, I did become something of an object of interest and it took time to adjust to this. I had hundreds of wonderful letters from the public from all over the country, voicing their appreciation of what *Coventry* had achieved and expressing great pride in our servicemen. A note from Miss Sandy Bennett in York was typical: 'I should like to say welcome home and thank you. My thanks are not only for what you and your brave men have done in the South Atlantic, but also for what you have done for me; never before in my lifetime have I been able to feel so proud to be British. I wish you well for the future.'

As well as letters, I received generous gifts, among them a crate of beer from Newcastle, some fresh salmon from Hertfordshire and a case of champagne from my naval tailor. (I even had a dog named after me in Dorset.) The salmon was sent to me by Arthur Rose, who had been the gunner's mate in the anti-aircraft cruiser *Coventry* in 1942 and survived her sinking. He knew what we had been through and wrote: 'This is a small offering, I know, but sufficient, perhaps, to remind you of our gratitude and admiration.' He needed to say nothing more.

It was heart-warming to receive such gifts and letters, especially those from the parents of *Coventry* sailors who thanked me for looking after their sons. D also received many letters of thanks for her care of the families. In the meantime, I found myself busy at home. There was a good deal to do around the house and garden, and there were the children to be looked after and taken to the local school each morning; indeed, it was their liveliness and their activities, which continued regardless, that did much to get me out of myself. We visited relations and friends, staying away with some of them at weekends, and all this, too, helped to prevent me from becoming too preoccupied and self-absorbed. All the same, D had a difficult time restoring my confidence and getting me away from thinking about the war. I was not aware of it at the time, but apparently I never stopped talking about it with various members of my family and friends. This was obviously a symptom of my still shocked state, even if it was also, I believe, a necessary part of the process of getting the experiences out of my system.

D recently recalled of this time: 'I could see that David's thoughts and feelings were entirely with the ship's company of *Coventry* and all that they had been through, and that the most important thing for him was to talk about it. Apart from me, concerned friends would visit and listen at length, absorbed by all that he had experienced. He would always try, when friends were with us, to get involved in their lives, but inevitably conversation slipped back to *Coventry*, and it was obvious that to let him talk as freely and as much as he wished was the best way to get help him through.

'I accompanied him to dinners around the country where he was invited to speak. This was quite stressful at times as I was never sure whether he would get through the speech without breaking down. When he left out certain passages, I knew he was struggling with his emotions. There is a kind of loneliness you can feel at times as a wife of someone returning from war. He is there and yet not there, and you know it is simply a question of patience and time. In the end, he got himself through the traumas entirely on his own, but with the support of family and friends around him. It was a wonderful moment when he emerged at the far end of his journey through his dark tunnel, and was back with me again.'

Many institutions and interested groups asked me to speak

about the war and I accepted a number of these invitations primarily because I still felt I owed it to my crew to tell the wider public what had happened. Audiences were riveted by the story – so much so that sometimes, when I had finished, there would be a few, very distinct moments of complete silence before any applause. This was quite unexpected and made me realize that the conflict was not just something to be played down as having been merely in the line of duty. The realization dawned that I really had taken part in a momentous event in the country's history and in a most remarkable maritime operation that few, if any, other nations could even have begun to undertake. I also began to accept that *Coventry* had been much at the centre of a drama that was well beyond the experience of most of those I found myself talking to on the subject. The ship's story was one of great hardship and stress borne bravely by professional and dedicated servicemen. At the very worst moments of the war, my sailors had been at their best: this was what was so much admired.

At the same time, I began to understand just how the whole nation had been transfixed by the great adventure running its dangerous course in the South Atlantic and had longed for its success every bit as much as it had reeled at the news of lives being lost. This had not been a television war in the modern sense, and only occasional glimpses of it were shown on the small screen: most people seem to recall watching footage of enemy air activity over Falkland Sound but little else until the recapture of Stanley. Information gathered by the few journalists with the British forces was necessarily controlled, and they were given only limited access to satellite communications to get their stories or pictures back to the UK. The public instead relied mainly on daily announcements from Ministry of Defence spokesmen, one of whose television manner was, by all accounts, especially sombre and often sent a shiver down the spine regardless of whether he was giving good news or bad.

But when the survivors of the war did return home, the interviews they gave were widely disseminated and clearly touched the whole country; this was, after all, the first time people really learnt about the horrors of the war and the truth of what had happened. It was not always what was said in these interviews or even how it was said which stayed with the public; it was these men's haunted expression, and the faraway look in their eyes as they relived some especially terrible moment. Some, like those in *Sheffield* or *Coventry*, *Ardent* or *Antelope*, had not only lost a ship; they had lost a whole family and a home. And now they were seeing it all again – the missiles, the bombs, the death of shipmates, the abandoning of the ship. These interviews told starkly of the tragedy of war yet they also illuminated the comradeship of men at arms. I know I had a similarly haunted air about me whenever I talked about *Coventry*. But again and again, like all the others, I just wanted to tell the story of my men and my ship.

Before going on holiday to Cornwall with my family – that same holiday I had told my sailors was booked for August – I had to attend a board of inquiry in Portsmouth. These boards are routine investigations to establish what lessons can be learnt from the sinking of a ship and what measures can be taken to prevent a repetition of such events. The findings confirmed that, given that *Coventry* was overwhelmed by bomber aircraft, there was nothing more that could have been done to save the ship. Much praise, however, was given to the crew in saving life. The chief lesson was that a ship should be equipped with weapons capable of defending it in such circumstances. This was, of course, an old lesson which had been learnt in previous wars, but peacetime economies often prevent the armed services from having all the weapons they need. As it was, we had planned and been trained for a different war, one in which we did not think we would be taking on bomber aircraft at such close range. But, as *Coventry* and other ships discovered, we were going to have to fight regardless, and to make the very best of what we had.

On 20 June 1982, D and I attended a memorial service in Coventry Cathedral when a congregation of 2,000 mourned the loss of the ship and nineteen of her crew. It was a very moving demonstration of the ties between the city and the ship. The service was attended by a number of my sailors and their families. Also present were the Chief of Defence Staff Admiral Lewin and his wife, who had, of course, launched *Coventry*, as well as other admirals representing the Admiralty Board, the Commander-in-Chief Portsmouth and the Flag Officer of the First Flotilla. This was the first of a number of memorial services which I was to attend, and these events were to prove a great help. Slowly but surely I was coming to terms with it all and putting the war behind me.

There was, at the very least, always the consolation of knowing that those of us who had been involved in the war had helped achieve something very significant – and Richard Luce had referred to this in a letter I received on my return. 'I believe,' he had written, 'very strongly that the sacrifice for the Islanders, our country and the world was and is worth it. I am sure your men did not lose their lives in vain – it was against aggression and for freedom and democracy. For the rest of your life you will be able to look back with pride at what you and your crew achieved for our country and that is something you should not forget.' This had been very reassuring to hear, and it was a message that I never hesitated to pass on to a number of *Coventry*'s bereaved families.

D and I duly had that holiday in Cornwall and it was marvellous. I did, however, feel a little uncomfortable when my daughters took to the beach wearing T-shirts emblazoned with the words 'Hart Dyke's Heroes. HMS *Coventry*. Falkland Isles 1982'. These T-shirts had been produced on our return in response to one of my broadcasts in *Coventry* and then offered for sale among the ship's company. Directly underneath the ship's name, against the background of a white ensign, was an elephant with two penguins at its feet stamping on a map of the Islands. The elephant is the main feature of the ship's crest, as it is of the city of Coventry's heraldic arms, symbolizing the strength of the city as a great manufacturing centre in the days of the Industrial Revolution. The creation of the T-shirts had been a flattering gesture, but all the same it made me uneasy to see my name displayed so publicly.

Later, D and I went off by ourselves to the mountains of Switzerland to escape the media attention and to catch up with each other again. We could hardly have been further from the sea, and I recall that I felt a world away from events in the South Atlantic. We stayed in a small but very comfortable establishment high up in the mountains and the only reminder of home was its name, the Hotel Miranda. We walked and talked, and the fresh air in my lungs gave me new energy, much of which would be needed for my new appointment working for the

Commander-in-Chief of the Fleet at Northwood as his warfare adviser. This was a busy job, involving, among other things, a major evaluation of all the lessons learnt from the Falklands War and then seeing ships modified and better equipped for any future conflicts. Close-range self-defence guns and missiles, for example, were speedily fitted in the remaining Type 42 destroyers. I hardly needed to argue the case for this expenditure – but how I wished I had had such weapons myself only a few weeks earlier.

In 2002, Margaret Thatcher was asked to contribute to *Memories of the Falklands*, a book edited by Iain Dale.

Nothing remains more vividly in my mind, looking back on my years in Number Ten, than the eleven weeks in the spring of 1982 when Britain fought and won the Falklands War. Much was at stake: what we were fighting for was not only the territory and the people of the Falklands, important though they were. We were defending our honour as a nation, and principles of fundamental importance to the whole world – above all, that aggressors should never succeed and that international law should prevail over the use of force. The significance of the war was enormous, both for Britain's self-confidence and for our standing in the world. Since the Suez fiasco in 1956, British foreign policy had been in one long retreat. We had come to be seen by both friends and enemies as a nation that lacked the will and capability to defend its interests in peace, let alone in war. Victory in the Falklands changed all that. Everywhere I went after the war, Britain's name meant something more than it had. The War also had real importance in relations between East and West. The Soviets had been firmly convinced that we would not fight for the Falklands, and that if we did fight, we would lose. We proved them wrong on both counts, and they did not forget it.

The Falklands conflict showed that, as always in war, it is training and skill which matter most. By and large, our opponents, mostly conscripts, were no match for our regular professional forces in these respects. But more important still is high morale. This is what makes men endure and display courage in times of fatigue and danger. This is what really counts, regardless of whether you enjoy an advantage in men and numbers or, as was the case with us in the Falklands, you do not. And the cultivation of morale depends on good leadership, discipline, comradeship and devotion to a just cause. The Task Force possessed all these ingredients off the Falkland Islands in 1982, while the enemy did not. In short, we had confidence, and he did not. This was what gave us our triumph.

Not long ago, a senior American admiral told me that he thought the Falklands War would go down in history as one of the most brilliant maritime operations of the twentieth century. Certainly, everything about it – the incredible speed with which the Task Force and all its specialist supporting shipping were assembled and manned; the ingenuity and improvisation which were displayed in modifying those ships and their equipment to meet a whole multitude of tasks – was remarkable. For his part, Sandy Woodward did all he possibly could with the forces at his disposal. Winston Churchill, a former First Lord of the Admiralty, had once famously remarked of Sir John Jellicoe, the commander of the Grand Fleet at the Battle of Jutland in 1916, that he was the only man on either side who could lose the First World War in an afternoon. Much the same might have been said of our admiral: he was the one man who could have lost the war in equally short order had anything happened to his carriers. But he protected them wisely and remained utterly steadfast, even at the worst moments. The lack of self-defence weapons on the ships, of airborne early warning and powerful air cover was no fault of his, even if we paid a corresponding price in ships sunk. Yet in spite of these serious shortcomings and losses, and in the face of formidable odds, we inexorably ground down the enemy's strength in the air and we successfully landed our troops and their equipment after transporting them across 8,000 miles of ocean. And we won. The American admiral was right: it had indeed been a brilliant operation, just as it was a brilliant victory.

If I were asked whether the loss of life and ships were worth the cost and the pain of so many, I would still unhesitatingly answer yes. This may not be of much comfort to those who lost husbands or sons or close relatives, but I firmly believe the benefits that victory brought, not only to the Falkland Islanders, but to the country and to democracy, were priceless. The alternative – not to fight – would have brought dishonour and lasting damage to the nation and the free world. Sadly, victory could never have been achieved without some sacrifice in lives and ships. Those who died did so fighting for freedom, the noblest of all causes. And to undertake that fight is the prime purpose of the British armed forces.

Our services possess a priceless inheritance, one which has given us men of great quality who have fought bravely down the ages. But the British fought no less bravely in the South Atlantic in 1982 than they had before or will fight in the future. I saw that for myself, which is why I still think I was so very privileged – and so very fortunate – to have been able to lead such men in action.

CHAPTER 15

FULL CIRCLE

I began work at Northwood at the end of the summer of 1982, being with Admiral Sir John Fieldhouse during his last few weeks before he moved to the Ministry of Defence, where he succeeded Admiral Sir Henry Leach as First Sea Lord. Sir John was later appointed Chief of the Defence Staff, a testament to the regard in which he was held by Mrs Thatcher and her government. Indeed, if any one person was the architect of our victory, it was John Fieldhouse.

Towards the end of the year, I was visited by Lieutenant-Commander Mike Kooner, the officer commanding the Fleet Diving Team, who had conducted an underwater survey of the wreck of *Coventry* lying on her side in 300 feet of water. The purpose of the survey had been to plan a dive on the ship, go inside, retrieve classified documents and make all the various warheads and explosives on board safe. A monitor was put on my desk so I could watch a video of the ship as the camera moved around it. We discussed the best way for the divers to get into the ship, by cutting a hole in the side, and what they would expect to find and where. I volunteered the combination number of the lock to the safe in my cabin which contained some sensitive material, and I also took the liberty of asking if, while they were there, the divers could look in the bottom left-hand drawer of my desk for my candlesticks and other pieces of silver.

I thought it unlikely they would be able to recover the silver as they had very limited time to achieve rather more important tasks in other parts of the ship – but they did. It was all delivered to me at home, lovingly cleaned, in pristine condition and completely unharmed after being submerged for six months. I have since had the two candlesticks engraved with the words 'Recovered from the wreck of HMS *Coventry*, Falkland Islands 1982' and they take pride of place on my dining-room table. The divers also brought up my sword and telescope, a hand-painted china bowl and a few other small items. Only the sword is unusable – it had rusted badly – and it now hangs on a wall at home looking rather the worse for wear.

To my even greater surprise, the diving team presented me one day in my office with the battle ensign we had been flying at the time of our last action, now washed, folded and pressed: it had still been streaming from its position on the mainmast hundreds of feet underwater before it was hauled down by the divers. But this was not all they found. One of the team looking around the ship, Leading Diver Dickie Daber, had glimpsed a bright object in a corner glinting in his light beam which, drifting in its wooden case, then floated into his hands as he moved close to it. It was, of course, the cross of nails. This too, quite undamaged, was delivered to me at home. There was only one thing to do with it, and I presented the cross back to Coventry

Cathedral in a simple ceremony for safekeeping until there was another *Coventry*. It was put on display in the Navy Room below the cathedral which now contained the memorials to two ships named *Coventry*.

In March 1984, I was thrilled to be asked to lay the keel of a new *Coventry* being laid down at Swan Hunter Shipbuilders in March 1984. Captain Sam Salt was also invited to do the same for a new *Sheffield* being built on the slipway alongside. This *Coventry*, a Type 22 frigate, was launched in 1986 and I would duly present the cross of nails to her when she was commissioned in Portsmouth in 1989, just as it had been presented to my ship. (Later, I was also able to present our battle ensign, which was framed behind glass and displayed in a prominent part of the ship.)

More than 700 guests attended the commissioning ceremony and the service of dedication, among them several sailors who had served with me in 1982 and relatives of some who had lost their lives. The Lord Mayor of Coventry attended as well as the cathedral's provost, the Very Reverend John Petty, and international director, Canon Paul Oestreicher. A new inscription had been put on the cross as a symbol of Coventry Cathedral's ministry of reconciliation: 'May this cross of nails be a reminder that Christ has broken down all human barriers. This Cross went down in the depths with HMS *Coventry* in the South Atlantic. In its presence remember all who died at the time, British and Argentinian, and all who grieve for them. And pray for the peace of the world.' Events had turned full circle. Both my own ship and its short but distinguished career were now well and truly part of history.

*

But in 1982, this was all in the future. Before the end of the year, a number of commemorative and celebratory occasions took place. In the autumn, there was a Falkland Islands service in St Paul's Cathedral, a victory parade and banquet in the City of London. There was some controversy over the service at St Paul's when the Archbishop of Canterbury, Dr Robert Runcie, preached a conciliatory sermon and remembered the dead of both sides in the conflict. Margaret Thatcher and a number of MPs were said to be angry about the service, believing that it should have been more patriotic and a better reflection of the nation's joy at the victory. Along with many other servicemen, I did not agree with this. I thought it was entirely right and proper to remember the bereaved of both countries and to hope for peace and reconciliation.

The military, especially those who have had a taste of war at first hand, are often far more forgiving of their enemies than politicians. The Navy's primary role, after all, is keeping the peace, preventing war, and it probably attracts people more interested in diplomacy than conflict. Young soldiers may join the Army for a good fight, but I think sailors join for other reasons, to see the world and also to represent their country abroad in a variety of ways. Nor do the military, least of all the Navy, much relish victory parades, especially when they are staged for glorification and political gain. I did not particularly enjoy watching the parade through the streets of the City of London, and nothing could have induced me to march.

There were two other occasions, however, both in October 1982, which meant a great deal more to me than parades or grand civic lunches. The first was a dinner in Nelson's flagship, HMS *Victory*, hosted by the Commander-in-Chief, Portsmouth,

Admiral Sir James Eberle. It was here that I met most of my fellow commanding officers of the Carrier Battle Group who had by now returned from the South Atlantic. I might have talked to them on the communications circuits or seen their ships through my binoculars, but this was the first time we had come face to face and could discuss our ships' many exploits.

In October 1805, after *Victory* had joined the fleet before the Battle of Trafalgar, Nelson had invited all his captains, nearly thirty of them, to dinner on board: he had done so on two separate occasions, offering hospitality to first one group of his commanders and then another. He had thus been able to tell them in person of his plan for the battle – the Nelson touch – and they had been both inspired and exhilarated by his simple but daring strategy, one they would execute to devastating effect. Now, 177 years later, our own band of twenty-one commanders were gathered in Nelson's dining room. The great man's presence was palpable as we sat around the polished table in the candlelit cabin with its white wooden walls and low ceiling supported by heavy oak beams. Indeed, he would have been completely at home in these familiar surroundings, unchanged since his own time on board. From the table, we could look through the gaps between elegant fluted columns to his day cabin in the aftermost part of the ship, where, by the windows, stood the round table at which he had written to Emma Hamilton for the last time and composed the final prayer on the morning of the battle.

The second occasion, in its way just as memorable, was when I was invited to be a guest of the Prime Minister at a dinner at Number Ten Downing Street. All the key players both at home and in the South Atlantic during the war were present and

Margaret Thatcher paid a generous tribute to them for their part in recapturing South Georgia and the Falkland Islands. There were nineteen officers present from the Royal Navy, Royal Marines and Merchant Navy, including all the senior naval commanders in London and Northwood. A number of officers from the other two services, together with principal ministers and civil servants, made up the total of sixty-six guests.

When I entered the reception room before dinner and was announced, Margaret Thatcher turned towards me and said in a loud voice, but in the manner of a friendly greeting, 'Ah, *Coventry*'. We then shook hands and she thanked me warmly. Our wives were invited to join us at a reception later, but not before the Prime Minister and Admiral Lewin had made brief speeches and she, the only woman present, had stood up and asked, to much laughter, 'Gentlemen, shall we join the ladies?' I have seen Margaret Thatcher on several occasions since and she has always been kind: she clearly felt the losses and sacrifices of the war very deeply.

But those dinners in *Victory* and Downing Street were almost a quarter of a century ago – a time when, like my ship's company, I still felt very raw about the war: immensely proud of what we had achieved but terribly saddened by our losses. In the intervening years, I have watched my daughters grow up and D work tirelessly to create an unusually beautiful garden in our home in Hampshire. I have left the Navy and pursued another career and other interests. It has made me a wiser and, perhaps, altogether a better person. Now I, too, find that the good memories of my time in *Coventry* are far stronger than the bad. I recall them often and, above all, I recall the people who won this war, especially those who never returned.

Coventry's own story would not be complete without mention of the memorial to the ship erected on Pebble Island in March 1983. Alan Fazackerley, a resourceful and courageous man who had helped save many from *Coventry* and was now serving in *Exeter*, was the prime mover here. He arranged, with help from Portsmouth dockyard, for the various parts to be put on board *Exeter* for assembly before she sailed for the South Atlantic. Then he led a small team of ex-*Coventry*s in building a cairn and erecting a cross on a spot which overlooks where the ship now lies off the northern coast of West Falkland.

The cross, made of varnished mahogany, stands some twenty-three feet high. Over the years, it has suffered at the hands of the weather but it is regularly maintained. The cairn was constructed with the large pebbles which give the island its name and into it are set two plaques. One is engraved with a roll of honour of the names of the ship's company who were lost and the other with the words:

HMS *COVENTRY*

SUNK 25 MAY 1982

IN MEMORY OF THE BRAVE MEN

WHO DIED THAT DAY

The memorial was dedicated in a service led by the Reverend Charles Howard, naval chaplain in the South Atlantic, and attended by all the *Coventry* survivors serving at that time in ships operating around the Islands and by the entire Pebble Island settlement. This small gathering paid tribute on a bare hilltop as they faced the cross and, beyond it, the sea. A cold wind rippled the rough grass and stirred the wreath of autumn flowers and evergreens which the Islanders had placed at the base of the cairn. Offshore, the destroyers *Cardiff* and *Exeter* steamed silently past.

Captain Hugh Balfour of *Exeter* wrote to me afterwards: 'It was a memorable moment and I think we all felt the same. Your team were very good and I think they are pleased and also glad that it is done . . . We thought of you, David.'

Two months later, on 25 May 1983, exactly a year after *Coventry*'s survivors had cheered *Broadsword* as they left her by boat on a dark night after a dramatic rescue, I was to receive a signal from the frigate, now back again in that all too familiar stretch of sea. The signal was short but eloquent: 'A wreath was laid today on the sea north of Pebble Island in remembrance of events one year ago. You cheered ship for us that evening. Three cheers for *Coventry*.'

Broadsword's words moved me then. They still move me now.

HMS *COVENTRY*
25 MAY 1982
ROLL OF HONOUR

Frank Armes

John Caddy

Paul Callus

Stephen Dawson

John Dobson

Michael Fowler

Ian Hall

Rodney Heath

David Ozbirn

Glen Robinson-Moltke

Bernard Still

Geoffrey Stockwell

David Strickland

Adrian Sutherland

Stephen Tonkin

Ian Turnbull

Philip White

Ian Williams

Kyu Ben Kwo

IN MEMORY

SHIP'S COMPANY 1982

Officers

R. J. Adams

R. P. W. Bell

P. A. Chivers

D. M. Cooke

T. R. Fletcher

A. C. Gwilliam

R. W. Hamilton

T. R. Harris

R. R. Heath

C. P. Holt

O. M. Howard

L. D. Jones

G. W. Lane

R. A. Lane

H. J. Ledingham

A. J. G. Miller

A. G. Moll

M. J. O'Connell

P. Plumridge

C. J. Pollard

A. A. Rich

M. P. Richardson

G. S. Robinson–Moltke

J. C. Troy

R. N. Tusting

D. Walton

I. M. Woodman

I. J. Young

Ratings

F. O. Armes	R. G. Brunton
S. Allen	R. T. Bryan
S. A. Allwood	N. C. Burchell
S. G. Andrews	P. J. Burke
S. W. Annable	M. E. Burkmar
M. T. Atkins	M. Burton
I. Atkinson	J. D. L. Caddy
B. W. Avery	P. B. Callus
A. W. Bagnall	J. D. Casey
W. Baker	D. Cheeseman
R. V. Barker	A. D. Church
K. J. Barton	G. Codognotto
D. P. Beeton	L. C. Colley
A. Bell	J. Collier
S. F. Bell	J. Collins
S. M. Bell	J. L. Cook
I. S. Bennett	M. Cook
P. S. Bennett	B. Cooper
T. R. Bennett	A. T. Crook
M. R. Berry	R. Crosby
S. Berry	W. Crowe
R. J. Birch	N. P. Cryer
K. Bishop	A. J. Cumper
K. R. Blenkharn	R. Curd
P. Bradford	M. Daniels
C. Briant	J. R. A. Davies
P. Briggs	M. P. S. Davies
M. Brown	R. D. Davies

J. Dawes

S. R. Dawson

M. D. Day

P. M. Dennis

A. Devine

M. Dilucia

J. K. Dobson

G. Dodgson

K. A. J. Douglas

D. P. Downey

P. Drummond

R. J. Drummond

J. F. Dunne

B. Durrant

C. M. Eames

P. T. Eastall

N. J. Edwards

R. D. Ellis

A. A. Estcourt

K. P. Everington

K. Fairclough

J. S. Fallon

A. F. Fazackerley

J. C. Findlay

P. R. Fisher

K. J. Fletcher

R. C. Fletcher

G. A. Flood

D. Flockton

J. Foster

M. G. Fowler

R. Galeozzie

G. Gilbert

M. H. Gough

M. A. Gould

P. Griffiths

N. Hackett

R. E. Hale

S. R. Hale

I. P. Hall

C. E. Halliday

J. W. Hardy

D. Harrison

M. Harrison

S. Harrison

P. W. Hazell

G. J. Heggie

J. W. Hemmings

N. C. Herriott

C. J. Higginson

A. R. Hill

T. C. Holder

R. S. Hopgood

D. Hornby

B. D. Houlders

L. P. Howard

C. Howe

M. J. Hughes

P. Hutton

S. Ingleby

P. Inman

M. R. Isaacs

M. R. E. Isaacs

D. James

R. Jenkins

R. M. Jenner

C. Johnson

M. W. Johnson

C. A. Jones

P. C. Jones

P. L. Jones

G. E. Kaunhoven

L. Kellett

F. J. Kelly

C. M. Kemp

N. P. Kemp

M. I. Kendall

M. C. Kerry

D. R. Kimber

G. King

N. D. Larsson

P. D. Leach

P. Legge

J. Leigh

T. A. Lendrum

D. R. Lewis

R. Livingston

W. M. Lovell

I. D. Luff

C. M. Mabbott

T. McCabe

P. M. McCartney

J. D. McCormack

G. S. McCutcheon

S. A. MacFarlane

P. Magnall

B. Mallinson

C. Manser

P. H. Marsh

J. Mason

J. A. Matthews

P. Matthews

S. Matthews

J. Maugham

J. Melia

J. Mew

T. P. Miles

P. T. Mills

K. Milner

C. D. Moore

S. P. Morgan

A. E. Morton

N. P. Murch

R. A. Nash

M. Newbold

M. L. Northeast

A. Nothers

D. R. Nunn

D. A. Nuttall

C. Neave

R. Newman	M. D. Scott
C. Norrell	V. A. Shane
G. M. Oram	J. W. Sharman
P. Ostler	R. Sharples
S. H. Overall	S. C. Shimmens
H. D. Owen	W. Skilleter
J. L. Oxford	B. Skipp
D. J. A. Ozbirn	C. S. Sluman
K. G. Palmer	A. C. Smith
M. Pattison	B. Smith
C. K. Phillips	P. D. Smith
G. Potter	T. G. Smith
S. Potts	J. A. Stevens
L. J. Pope	D. M. Stevenson
P. Ray	J. S. W. Stevenson
A. J. Reece	A. Stewart
T. Reef	B. J. Still
P. Richardson	G. L. T. Stockwell
P. T. Richardson	D. A. Strickland
C. A. Ridgill	K. Stuart
P. K. Roberts	M. Stuart
P. Robson	S. Sudworth
S. D. Rouse	S. L. Sugden
G. D. Rowe	A. D. Sunderland
R. L. Rowell	T. A. Sutton
W. D. Rumsey	S. Swords
J. Russell	G. J. Sylvester
M. Rutherford	M. H. Taylor
B. C. Savage	J. Taylour
T. Sawyer	A. Thomas

F. N. Thomas	W. S. Welbury
H. G. Thomas	G. Weldon
P. Thomas	R. F. Whitbread
F. A. Thompson	J. R. White
I. Tilbury	P. J. White
T. Tominey	P. P. White
P. Tomlinson	A. Whitlock
S. Tonkin	M. W. Whitney
T. M. Trevarthen	G. S. Williams
I. E. Turnbull	I. R. Williams
J. R. Turner	K. Wilson
J. Twyman	M. Winch
D. M. Tyson	A. Winsor
A. S. Urban	A. Wood
B. Wakefield	D. M. Wood
J. S. Walker	J. Woodhouse
S. Walker	A. Woodruff
E. Walock	S. J. Woolham
S. R. Wason	N. G. Wright
R. S. Webb	N. Young

Note: After so many years it has been difficult to compile an accurate list of those who served in *Coventry* during the Falklands War and the author apologizes for any errors or omissions. He would wish to be advised of any inaccuracies, particularly omissions, so as to be able to set the record straight.

EPILOGUE

Inevitably I will have drawn attention to myself by writing this book and would therefore like the reader to remember that everyone else in *Coventry*, as well as those in the other ships that were sunk or damaged in action, will have similar stories to tell and enduring memories of traumatic events. We survivors would not for one moment, however, be looking for sympathy but rather an understanding of the nature of war and its effects on people – both those doing the fighting and the families at home. Particularly, we should remember those who lost close relatives and friends: their war was no easier and its effects on them were greater. For us it was 'life in a blue suit'. We were doing what we were trained to do and, despite the strains and the violence, willing and proud to be doing it. War is what the Royal Navy does when it has to. We go forward regardless of the odds, which is what makes our ships worth more than anyone else's. And on some days your luck can run out.

HMS *COVENTRY* (D118)

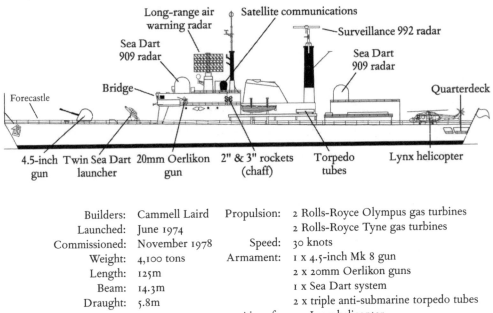

Long-range air warning radar

Satellite communications

Surveillance 992 radar

Sea Dart 909 radar

Sea Dart 909 radar

Bridge

Quarterdeck

Forecastle

4.5-inch gun

Twin Sea Dart launcher

20mm Oerlikon gun

2" & 3" rockets (chaff)

Torpedo tubes

Lynx helicopter

Builders:	Cammell Laird	Propulsion:	2 Rolls-Royce Olympus gas turbines
Launched:	June 1974		2 Rolls-Royce Tyne gas turbines
Commissioned:	November 1978	Speed:	30 knots
Weight:	4,100 tons	Armament:	1 x 4.5-inch Mk 8 gun
Length:	125m		2 x 20mm Oerlikon guns
Beam:	14.3m		1 x Sea Dart system
Draught:	5.8m		2 x triple anti-submarine torpedo tubes
		Aircraft:	1 x Lynx helicopter

BOMB DAMAGE

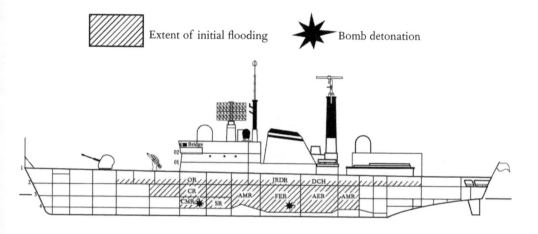

Extent of initial flooding   Bomb detonation

OR:	Operations Room
CR:	Computer Room
CMR:	Conversion Machinery Room
SR:	Store Rooms
AMR:	Auxiliary Machinery Room

JRDH:	Junior Rates Dining Room
FER:	Forward Engine Room
DCH:	Damage Control Headquarters
AER:	After Engine Room

OPERATIONS ROOM

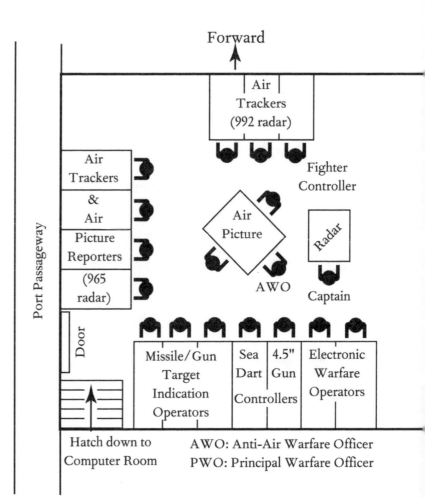

Forward

Air Trackers (992 radar)

Fighter Controller

Air Trackers & Air Picture Reporters (965 radar)

Air Picture

Radar

AWO

Captain

Port Passageway

Door

Missile/Gun Target Indication Operators

Sea Dart | 4.5" Gun Controllers

Electronic Warfare Operators

Hatch down to Computer Room

AWO: Anti-Air Warfare Officer

PWO: Principal Warfare Officer

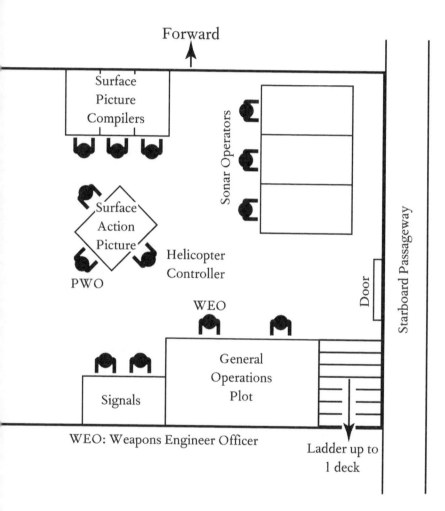

Forward

Surface Picture Compilers

Sonar Operators

Surface Action Picture

PWO

Helicopter Controller

WEO

Signals

General Operations Plot

Door

Starboard Passageway

Ladder up to 1 deck

WEO: Weapons Engineer Officer

257

BIBLIOGRAPHY

Barnett, Correlli, *Engage the Enemy More Closely: the Royal Navy in the Second World War*, Hodder & Stoughton, 1991

Bennett, Geoffrey, *Coronel and the Falklands*, B. T. Batsford Ltd, 1962

Clapp, Michael, and Ewen Southby-Tailyour, *Amphibious Assault Falklands: the Battle of Carlos Water*, Leo Cooper, 1996

Critchley, Michael, (ed.), *Falklands – Task Force Portfolio*, Maritime Books, 1982

Dale, Iain, (ed.), *Memories of the Falklands*, Politico's Publishing, 2002

Ethell, Jeffrey, and Alfred Price, *Air War South Atlantic*, Sidgwick & Jackson, 1983

Hastings, Max, and Simon Jenkins, *The Battle for the Falklands*, Michael Joseph, 1983

Martin, Middlebrook, *Operation Corporate: the Falklands War, 1982*, Viking, 1985

Oakley, Derek, *The Falklands Military Machine*, Spellmount Limited, 1989

Underwood, Geoffrey, *Our Falklands War: the Men of the Task Force Tell their Story*, Maritime Books, 1983

Winton, John, *Air Power at Sea – 1945 to today*, Sidgwick & Jackson, 1987

Winton, John, (ed.), *Signals from the Falklands: the Navy in the Falklands Conflict*, Leo Cooper, 1995

Woodward, Admiral Sir John ('Sandy'), with Patrick Robinson, *One Hundred Days: the Memoirs of the Falklands Battle Group Commander*, HarperCollins, 1992

INDEX